THE WRITING OF MODERN FICTION

THE WRITING OF
MODERN FICTION

Robert Somerlott

THE WRITER, INC. / PUBLISHERS

BOSTON

Library of Congress Catalog Card Number: 71-188590
ISBN: 0-87116-068-4

PRINTED IN THE U.S.A.

CONTENTS

FOREWORD

I know a lecture hall where many beginning writers gather to hear the advice of established professional authors. On the wall hangs a large sign, a warning which also happens to be the title of a good novel by Hannah Green. It says: *"I never promised you a rose garden."*

This book comes with those words of caution. Your career or avocation as a fiction writer will probably not be a bed of roses. But it needn't be a bed of nails, either. An intelligent approach based on the experiences of others will lessen the difficulties.

No attempt is made here to present a single, all-inclusive theory of modern fiction writing. I am profoundly suspicious of people who offer a "step-by-step, never-fail system from first idea to published story." Exact recipes with measured ingredients and numbered instructions may work well in cookery, and precise blueprints are vital in the construction business. But successful fiction can neither be cooked up nor measured with a protractor. It is not produced by doggedly obeying one set of rigid "rules." Every writer must find the way that works best for *him*, and no two writers are exactly alike. Nor is it true that "any fool can do it," although I know a few who have.

This work is largely, but not entirely, a problem-solving book. Its main concern is with the craft of today's fiction, and it deals with specific difficulties authors encounter in their work. Hopefully it is also a guide to self-editing and self-criticism. No one finds it easy to ferret out the weaknesses in his own work; perhaps the following pages will suggest where to start looking for mistakes.

There are no smooth, swift expressways to guaranteed success in modern fiction writing. But certainly one can find shortcuts and ways of avoiding detours. I hope this book will remove some roadblocks and mark the route more clearly.

—Robert Somerlott

THE WRITING OF MODERN FICTION

~ 1 ~

FACTS OF LIFE

"WRITERS write."

This obvious truth, uttered forty-odd years ago by Alexander Woollcott, is profound. Full understanding of it is the first step toward a career in modern fiction.

"Writers write." They write beautifully, badly, or indifferently—but always they put words on paper. Often they write while bedeviled by interruptions and demands on their time: William Faulkner produced *Sanctuary* between furnace-stokings when he was a schoolhouse janitor. Even physical sufferings and handicaps have not halted the work of authors: An extreme example is the case of Christy Brown of Dublin who is so crippled that he can type only with the little toe of his left foot. Yet he completed *Down All My Days*, a novel which has been translated into every European language.

When I meet a group of fledgling authors, I have no way of predicting which ones are destined for success. But it's easy to recognize some who are doomed to failure. They are the "writers" who do not really write at all—or

1

who write so little that it counts for nothing. They are re-
pelled by the idea of working on a fixed schedule, and the
fact that most *real* writers toil day after day to produce
a roughly set number of words teaches no lesson to these
dabblers.

They talk glibly about writing. They love to expound
an idea for a novel or regale you with a half-formed notion for a short story. Many of these hopeless hopefuls en-
roll in classes, attend writers' conferences, and read such
books as this one. But, since they seldom put pen to
paper, their efforts and their money are wasted. No
teacher in the world, no book ever written can help a beginner who will not help himself by actually writing
down words, then more words, then still more.

Dilettantes who merely study and who consider writing as little as a thousand words a month a major
achievement will possibly learn a great deal *about* fiction
writing, but will never know the thing itself. Of course,
they will avoid the hard work required to master any
craft. And they will miss the joy of creation, the pride
and fulfillment that are among the greatest rewards of
producing effective fiction.

Not long ago at a dinner party an elderly lady said to
me, "You know, I've lived a most unusual life! If I'd written down my experiences, they would have made a fascinating novel. But with three children and a husband to
care for, I never had time."

I gave her the polite, false smile that all writers display
when they hear these familiar remarks. I murmured
something vague about how interesting her book would
have been, about its undoubted success. A social lie, of
course. The fact that she "never had time" proved that
she was no writer. A real author, a woman with the

ambition and dedication necessary for success, would have *made* the time.

It wouldn't have been easy: hours snatched here and there, strict limitation of demands made on her by her family and friends. She would have had to be ruthless about rationing her time. When it comes to the vital question of whether or not a writer shall be allowed to write, ruthlessness may be necessary.

Every successful author I know is unyielding about his working time. A few, who have the dispositions of saints, try to conceal their annoyance when interrupted, but usually it is safer to stroll into a lion's den than to intrude upon a laboring writer.

Outsiders do not always understand this. Recently my work was halted by the persistent jangling of the telephone. "Hello!" I snarled.

"Oh, I hope I'm not calling at a bad time," said the woman on the phone, detecting a certain hostility in my heavy breathing.

"Not at all," I said icily. "I was only writing."

"Good." She was greatly relieved. "I was afraid I'd interrupted your lunch."

I could have strangled her. If my soup gets cold and my salad warm because of a mealtime call, I may be irritated. But breaking in upon the sanctity of my working time is a personal assault.

The dilettante writer always has time to chat, to take a coffee or a cocktail break, to serve on committees, or to haunt bistros where other non-writing writers gather to assure each other that they are all future James Joyces. To such people writing is not work but a way of avoiding work. It is quite futile and would be tragic if these talkers really cared about writing. But they don't— or they would sit down and do it.

Writers write. They continue working even in the face of discouragement. All professions are cursed with Cassandras, but the field of fiction is absolutely rife with crepe-hangers and calamity howlers. The young writer, who needs hope and confidence above all things, hears instead the wails of pessimists.

"Fiction is dead," they say. "Nobody reads novels any more. The short story is almost extinct. Everything's hopeless."

Such gloom is enough to freeze the creative blood of any author, and in fiction writing a negative attitude is the prelude to failure.

This book is about writing, not selling. Nevertheless, if you are a beginning author who hopes to create fiction, you have every reason to ask, "Am I training myself for a dying profession? Why struggle if all doors are barred to me?"

Let's take a brief but honest look at the state of fiction today. Is there reason for despair?

It would be pleasant to dismiss all negative comments as nonsense, but the Cassandras have a grain of truth in their moaning, even though it is one grain in a wheat-field.

Success in any of the arts has always been difficult and uncertain. There have never been audiences large enough to support all the people who want to become actors, nor enough patrons for the work of all painters and sculptors. Creative writers face the same competitive struggle. Not everyone will triumph. After all, there is a limited number of novels and stories published, and Nobel Prizes are somewhat scarce.

This is no cause for despair, unless you despair of life itself. An artist faces extraordinary difficulties, but his position is by no means unique. Thousands of would-be physicians are never admitted to medical schools or are forced to drop out without finishing; the United States Chamber of Commerce reports that the vast majority of small businesses fail in the first year. Yet no one uses these gloomy facts to discourage people with ambition from trying to enter business or medicine. Writing is like any other field: there will be winners and losers. (You already have one great advantage. You know that writers *write*, and you will apply this knowledge while many of your competitors continue chatting about the glorious things they will produce at a vague future date.)

"Of course success in fiction was never easy," say the pessimists. "But nowadays it has become impossible. We live in a special time."

I submit, not very respectfully, that this view is ridiculous. Fiction, far from being dead, has never been more lively and exciting. The obituaries for the novel one reads must come as great surprises to Saul Bellow, Gore Vidal, Joyce Carol Oates, Norman Mailer, and scores of other authors whose works reach a constantly expanding audience.

It is true that fiction has changed greatly in the last decade, and such changes will continue—as they always have. There is, for instance, the "nonfiction novel" exemplified by Capote's *In Cold Blood,* and in another way by Mailer's *Armies of the Night.* This form is not so revolutionary as publicity has suggested; it has a legion of literary predecessors. But even if this innovation is not so very radical, it remains a sign of healthy expansion and growth.

Today's fiction writer enjoys a freedom of expression unknown to earlier generations. He is seldom bedeviled by outright censorship; he is not bound by the straitjacket of formula writing; if he wishes to experiment with new forms, new methods, he will find a far more receptive and less prejudiced audience than James Joyce and Gertrude Stein faced throughout most of their careers.

Certain avant-garde prophets claim that the printed word, as art and entertainment, will be replaced by other media—tape cassettes are frequently mentioned. If so, you may rejoice at the good fortune of the recording companies, and sympathize with the plight of printers. But as a fiction writer you will not be affected. Whether royalties come from tapes or books is of little consequence to you, for a storyteller can communicate through the ear as well as the eye. They did in Homeric days, in medieval times; and still today in the Orient the teller of tales is a beloved figure. Rest assured that good storytellers will be in demand. Media and techniques may change, but humanity's love of an exciting narrative remains constant.

The one area of fiction writing where the pessimists seem to have a plausible case involves the short story. Some magazines featuring short fiction have foundered, while others have reduced space allotted to fiction. As a result, many writers have had to adjust to a shrinking market and a few have retired altogether.

But for a new author this situation is not as disastrous as it seems at first glance. With exceptions, each of the defunct magazines had its own "stable of fiction writers," or at least its favorites. The same by-lines appeared over and over, year after year. Since admission to this charmed circle was always rare, today's fledgling writer should not feel that his career is doomed by the passing of some of the great, old magazines. The narrower market is a handicap, but not a fatal one. One must simply rise to meet the competition for space in the major magazines or, failing that, write for markets not so restricted.

The areas of magazine publishing where beginners have traditionally found a welcome are still open and thriving. Most of these periodicals are not glamorous, celebrated, or rich. But a new writer cannot afford snobbery.

There are the "little magazines," the literary magazines offering greater rewards in honor than in cash. Although no full-time professional author could survive by writing solely for these publications, their value is not to be underestimated. Sometimes they open the road to grants, awards, and fellowships. Success in the literaries attracts the attention of agents and book publishers— then there is always the chance that a story will be chosen for a major anthology. Newcomers with something fresh to say and a vital way of saying it are sought by these publications.

At the other end of the literary spectrum, you have the confession magazines. They gobble up more than a million words of fiction annually, and have become much more literate, much closer to the mainstream of fiction than they once were. They require a special emphasis, but the techniques of good narrative apply. Confessions form an important part of popular culture and, surprising as it may be to some people, their editors have shown themselves highly alert to social change and controversy. They were accepting stories dealing with interracial marriage and even homosexuality at a time when such themes were taboo in supposedly more "advanced" magazines. More important to you, these editors are forever on the lookout for capable new writers.

Mystery-suspense magazines will never make anyone rich, but these publications are another comparatively open market. Sometimes the rewards are astonishing. One of my stories, a short piece with the unlikely title

"Do Your Christmas Shoplifting Early," was nearly accepted by several prestigious magazines as a humorous novelty. They all decided it was "too odd," and it ended being published by *Ellery Queen's Mystery Magazine*. I was delighted to see it in print and grateful for a less than munificent check. Then a television producer read the story. He optioned it at a price of five times the original payment, and I recently learned that "Shoplifting," already translated for several foreign publications, will appear in a new American anthology. "Modest markets" are not to be ignored!

Science fiction, not long ago, was such a financially unrewarding field that it should have been declared an economic disaster area. Also, with brilliant exceptions, it was often literarily sterile. Today this area of fiction still has ups and downs, but there is an evolution upward in both quality and payment. Nowadays science fiction's only literary limitation is the ability of the author, for its readers are intelligent and critical. There is every reason for new writers to have hope in this field.

Then there are always the high-paying, mass circulation magazines—*The New Yorker, Esquire, Playboy,* and others. If you are a beginner, the odds against acceptance are great, but why not aim for the best? You have nothing to lose except postage.

Be prepared for rejection. Console yourself with the fact that all writers have gone through it, and even famous professionals frequently receive thumbs-down verdicts on some new work. The late John Steinbeck once told me a story that should offer comfort to all writers. He was at the height of his fame, had just won the Nobel Prize, and there wasn't a magazine in America that wouldn't have accepted anything he wrote. If he had chosen to submit his laundry list, some editor would have bought it just to have the celebrated Steinbeck name on next month's cover. At this time he wrote a short story, confident of its success. But his agent of many years returned it to him with a tactful but firm message: the new work was substandard and its publication would be a literary embarrassment. Steinbeck, after recovering from the initial shock, reread the story and ruefully decided that his agent was absolutely right. A few years later he could laugh about the rejection. I doubt that he laughed when it happened. What author could?

You can soften rejection-slip shock by always having several things in circulation at once. That way all your hopes will not be pinned to a single work.

Every published writer was once an unpublished one; every great name in fiction was once unknown.

And how did these authors get their start? By sitting down and writing. Because, whatever else they do, writers write!

~ 2 ~

LEARNING YOUR CRAFT

"WRITING can't be taught. Either you've got the talent or you haven't."

This destructive notion, which one hears repeated constantly, must be drummed out of the mind before we can get down to the practical business of writing. It is a doubly dangerous belief: First, it may prevent a young writer from seeking instruction which would help him. Second, there is an implied discouragement in the words. If a novice sends out half a dozen stories and all are rejected, what is he to think of his future? He doesn't appear to have that mysterious "talent" at the moment, and the sad corollary of "It can't be taught" is "It can't be learned."

The can't-be-taught view has been demolished many times by both argument and example. Teachers, wielding pens like lances, charge into the fray girded by outrage and righteousness. Yet the hydra grows new heads, and the can't-be-taught belief persists in many minds.

Why? My years spent as a learner, writer, and teacher have convinced me that this fallacy survives because there is truth in it—truth misunderstood and distorted, but still truth:

1. Fiction writing can't be taught to reluctant or captive students. Even a pupil who detests arithmetic eventually masters the multiplication tables if he has normal intelligence. But fiction writing cannot be learned by rote. Ambition and great love of the work are necessary.

I remember a disheartening class I attended in college. Of more than a dozen students only two of us had the least expectation of writing professionally. The others were fugitives from required courses in English. They thought "Creative Writing" might be more interesting than lectures on Chaucer or Dickens. (It wasn't.) The elderly professor sternly discouraged "commercialism." He held all "slick" magazines in utter contempt, sneered at science fiction and men's adventure stories. Confession magazines, the largest publishers of short stories in the world, were beneath mention, and if he ever read a mystery story, I'm sure it was in the sealed privacy of his bedroom. Naturally, he was quite unaware of the existence of popular culture.

Instruction was always slanted toward the majority of the class—all future attorneys, architects, or engineers. This was *not* a course for potential writers. Yet I cannot blame the professor except for his narrowness. He knew the futility of trying to teach even the mechanics of an art to those who don't expect to become artists. If a student produced a couple of short stories and a few brief sketches during the term, his homework was pronounced satisfactory. Of course, no writer can learn much while writing so little.

Although many colleges today offer excellent classes and workshops in writing, in others, courses in fiction writing remain the stepchildren of the English Departments and are taught from the cynical point of view that most students will never become writers. Such classes and such teachers contribute powerfully to the writing-can't-be-taught myth.

2. Instruction that helps one writer may fail entirely with another. Fiction writing is taught in various ways: through books, magazines, correspondence courses, and in classrooms. The teachers share broad areas of agreement, but each one has his own method, his own personality. This is true in all fields, but in the arts it looms as an enormously important factor. Even an excellent teacher may not be able to help a certain talented student because the two are literarily incompatible. If they lack mutual respect and appreciation, the result is not learning but a series of pitched battles. Painters and sculptors have been aware of this for centuries. Most of them move from one master to another while learning their craft.

Sometimes a difficulty of learning is not personalities but methods. One well-known teacher, who is also an excellent writer and editor, advocates what he calls "Finger Exercises." The student-writer takes a passage from some good author's work and imitates it, using exactly the same number of words, identical sentence structure, parallel placement of adjectives, verbs and other parts of speech.

Such exercises, which I find deplorable, have apparently helped certain students taught by certain instructors. At one time I repressed my misgivings and tried the system with a group of young writers who quickly proved themselves adept at working out these acrostics. But did their own writing improve? I did not think so. They probably learned *something* just because they were dealing with words. Still, I felt that the time spent in puzzle-solving could have been used better otherwise. I also suspected that the approach led to a mistaken attitude: it ignored the enormous part the writer's own emotions play in fiction.

Yet I cannot flatly deny that this method, properly presented and with due cautions given, might aid some people. To me, it is like trying to perform ballet while buckled into a steel corset. But I realize that there is no single "right way" for everybody.

3. A talented writer, working alone, will discover by trial and error almost everything any writing course or self-help book teaches. This is absolutely true—and what a waste of time it involves! The beginner who avoids all advice and instruction (since "writing can't be taught") is foolishly extending his term of apprenticeship.

Certainly the perceptive, self-critical newcomer will eventually stumble onto the known techniques of narrative writing. And no technique has been "learned" until the writer makes effective use of it on his own. But an experienced person can rather quickly explain innumerable things that a lonely beginner would discover on his own only after immense effort. Why try to figure out the basic formulas of plane geometry when they have been known for centuries? It's easier to learn that the area of a circle equals its squared radius times 3.1416 by looking in a book than by experimenting for years with dinner plates and coins. But even this simple bit of knowledge is not really *yours* until you have practiced it. The same thing is true in writing.

4. Instruction, after a certain amount of time, often produces di-

minishing returns. Discovery of basic elements of fiction as a craft breaks upon some new writers like the dawning day. Such a writer will quickly learn to detect the worst faults in his own work, will soon find out that some ideas have little potential as stories while others are promising. Then progress becomes slower, the task more difficult. A writer then needs time to write and to apply the principles he has intellectually learned but not emotionally mastered.

(Be prepared, by the way, for a sort of mid-season emotional slump. Many a writer, after a few months of studying his craft, suddenly wails, "I'm getting worse, not better!" He is suffering from growing pains, and has simply become more demanding, far more self-critical.)

All good fiction writers are "perennial students" because they are constantly learning. They continue to find stimulation from life, literature, and from meeting and talking with other writers, editors, and critics. They come across fresh ideas and new viewpoints in periodicals devoted to writing. But classroom work, unless devoted almost entirely to direct criticism of manuscripts, becomes less rewarding as time goes by. A student writer should expect guidance and help; he should be pointed in the right direction and set on the easiest path. Then he makes most of his journey alone.

Another form of group learning should be mentioned. In countless places, writers gather to read and discuss their manuscripts. These literary bands range from well-organized pen clubs to informal get-togethers in somebody's apartment. I have observed many such meetings, and my reactions have varied from great admiration to shocked embarrassment combined with pity.

At their best, these discussion groups stimulate a writer, arouse his competitive instincts, and provide sound criticism. Fine and even great writing has been inspired by talk at private "salons," in sidewalk cafés, and famously in taverns. Also, a writers' club or circle helps counteract the solitude in which an author must work. Apart from being helpful, these groups provide an oasis in the Sahara.

But if you are a beginning fiction writer, you must be careful about the company you keep. Somerset Maugham once said, "People ask you for criticism, but they only want praise." Often writers meeting together succumb to this powerful desire. Their gatherings can disintegrate into pointless mutual admiration societies: the sloppier the writing, the more gushing the praise. Encouragement is necessary, but a writer basking in flattery is not spurred to greater effort. On the contrary, he is lulled by the honeyed words of people who expect their own ration of honey in return. No respectable writer would be found dead or alive in such an orgy of congratulations more than once! Happily, most pen clubs are sincere.

At the opposite pole are groups dominated by the strong personalities—usually frustrated authors—who take fiendish delight in savagely attacking the works of others. Their purpose, often unconscious, is to prove their own brilliance by demolishing the efforts of fellow writers. These self-appointed critics should be avoided as one would shun the pesthouse. They cannot help you, and they may well destroy you.

Some people will ask just anybody—quite literally *anybody*—to read and evaluate their work. Worse, they accept the subsequent verdict without considering the source. One expects Joe's wife to think Joe's writing is "perfectly marvelous," and many of Joe's friends will agree, even at the price of honesty. Such biased praise, like biased criticism, will teach Joe nothing.

In brief, the novice writer who can obtain formal instruction in fiction should certainly do so. But he may
have to do some shopping around before he finds help
that is practical and inspiring *for him*. He can learn much
from a good teacher, but he will be "given" nothing. The
same applies to all gatherings of writers, whether in classrooms or not. And neither instruction nor discussion is a
substitute for the actual work of writing. They must all go
together. To put it another way:

"Can you play the piano?"

"No, but I took lessons for ten years."

"Did you ever practice?"

"Why should I have practiced? After all, I was taking
lessons."

~ 3 ~

"WHAT DO I WRITE ABOUT?"

YOU want to write a story—or a novel. A dozen un-
formed or half-formed ideas are shimmering in your
imagination; groups of shadowy characters hover at the
edge of your consciousness. There are so many things to
write about, so many tales to be told!

But your time is limited. You cannot develop every notion for fiction that flashes across your mind. Which subjects should you pursue at once, and which should be put
low on your list of priorities? In other words: "What do I
write about?"

Often there seems to be no question. A compelling idea
seizes you and you know, or at least you think you know,
that this is *it*. You must create fiction from this particular
stroke of inspiration.

When such an idea lends itself to the short story form,
obviously the thing to do is to write it at once. But if it is
to be a novel, second thoughts are needed. Writing a
novel demands time and stamina. It is foolhardy to hur-
tle ahead like a fire engine because of what may prove to

17

be a false alarm. Even "inspiration" should be carefully examined.

Many authorities have given writers advice about the choice of subject matter. By far the most common dictum is "Write about what you know." This has been said so many times that it has become almost a First Commandment. All young writers believe it, even though they violate the creed in practice.

At risk of being stoned as a heretic, I should like to say that "Write about what you know," unless interpreted broadly, is a dubious First Commandment. Of course, it applies fully to historians and biographers, and one fervently wishes that certain travel-guide writers and journalists kept the Law with more zeal than they often show. But fiction is a different matter, and often "knowing" has little to do with its creation.

The very authors who pronounce the Commandment are quick to violate it. Somerset Maugham, if I may again quote that slickest of all smooth writers, says in one of his introductions, "It is easier to write of what you know than of what you don't." Yet that same gentleman, early in his career, deliberately set his novel *Then and Now* in the Italian Renaissance. He admits he knew little enough about this period, but was confident that his readers knew even less. As a beginner, he felt more at ease handling his characters if he placed them against an historical backdrop, correctly divining that readers demand less realism from a hero dressed in a doublet than from one in an everyday business suit.

The historical novel or the story set in an exotic, unknown locale has its own peculiar demands, but the problem of believability is somewhat reduced. If a freebooter on the Spanish Main does not behave in a completely plausible way, we, as readers, are likely to forgive the author. "After all, things were different back then."

Remoteness does increase believability, whether the distance is in time or space. This is one very good reason why almost all romantic novels of suspense, the so-called "gothics," take place on distant islands, isolated coasts, or are set in a past century.

Naturally the author must know a good deal about the background and period he selects. If possible, his manuscript should be checked by an expert. But the writer's own knowledge need not be all-encompassing and profound; if he is writing an historical work, he cannot possibly know the background from his own experience, and he must therefore research it.

My second novel, *The Inquisitor's House,* is largely set in Mexico at the turn of the century. I was very familiar with the landscape and had lived in most of the places I described. Also, I did extensive historical research. As a result, I now have a mental attic crammed with facts and oddities of Mexico *circa* 1900. But I am decidedly not an authority; I merely know more than most people do about the subject. The book, I am convinced, succeeded not because of my knowledge of the era and locale, but because I deeply felt the characters and atmosphere.

Since this is so often the case, I propose that the First Commandment, "Write what you know," should be amended. "Write what you *feel*" is a better rule.

Creating fiction is first of all an emotional process. Intellect, taste and all the other qualities that combine in the critical faculty are constantly at work—especially during revision of first drafts. Critical judgment may be the governess of good fiction, but emotion is its father. If several story ideas suggest themselves to you, choose first the one that touches your feelings most strongly. The kind of emotion aroused does not matter—rage, humor, scorn, love, or any combination of feelings. Waste no time in writing about a situation that fails to move you in one way or another, no matter how familiar you are with the characters and background.

Emotion power

In recent years I have seen the results of several experiments conducted by Thomas Scott, a writer and teacher of nonfiction writing. Mr. Scott asked a group of students to make a list of five first names they thoroughly detested. Next, each student underlined the name he hated above all others. Then came a surprise assignment: write a personal essay telling why that particular name aroused such loathing.

The results were nothing less than astonishing. Never had work of such uniformly high quality been produced by this group! The most pedestrian writer among them suddenly waxed eloquent as he lashed out at a childhood enemy. One beginner created a beautiful and touching piece in which she revealed that the most hated name was her own.

To make sure that this upsurge in quality was not an accident, the experiment was repeated with two other groups. Both times the average level of work soared.

Most of these students lacked the technique and experience to sustain power for long. But at least briefly they added cubits to their writing statures because they were buoyed up by an uncomplicated and deeply-felt emotion. The surprise element was important, too. The writers were lured into revealing a hatred without realizing they would have to write about it. There was no chance to reject a character as "too ordinary" or "too personal."

Although writing good fiction is more complex than the assignment just described, the psychological factor at work still applies. Important though it is for an author to know the place, persons, and society he deals with, our proposed First Commandment still remains: Write what you feel.

Life-story novels: Watch out!

We have suggested that you should attempt to tell stories about things you feel deeply. And, if you are like most writers, your fiction will always contain some elements and incidents that are in a broad sense autobiographical. If this is so, doesn't it follow that your first major project should be the story of your own life fictionalized? After all, we all love ourselves (or at least the best part of ourselves), and who among us does not have some symptoms of an Old Oaken Bucket complex: "How dear to my heart are the scenes of my childhood . . . ."

The impulse to write fictionalized autobiography is almost universal among beginning writers, especially among those who think of themselves as "serious." At first glance this seems to be a logical approach to a writing career. All fiction can, in one way or another, be traced back to experience—although the "experience" may be only imagined, not lived. And is there anything you know so well as the events of your own life? The arguments for beginning your work with an autobiographical novel sound very convincing on paper.

There is only one thing wrong with such a plan: *it seldom works.* Books of this type, when done in the traditional chronological form, are almost never published, and on the occasions when one somehow worms its way into print, the public usually reacts with a resounding silence.

To avoid confusion, we'll use the terms "autobiographical" and "biographical" as little as possible, for we are not talking about fictionalized biographies of historical persons. Such works as *The Passions of the Mind* (about Sigmund Freud) and *Moulin Rouge* (about Toulouse-Lautrec) are in another category. The life-story novel we refer to here is more or less contemporary in setting and realistic in intent. It usually starts with the birth or early youth of the leading character and recounts the events of a life year by year—cradle to grave, or at least kindergarten to altar. Among the many famous examples are *Tom Jones, Of Human Bondage,* the Studs Lonigan trilogy, *David Copperfield* and *Moll Flanders.* These works, while very different from each other, all follow a familiar pattern: they are life-stories told chronologically—childhood, adolescence, maturity.

This type of structure, surviving in the classics, is out of favor today. There are exceptions, but if you examine lists of best-selling or prize-winning novels of recent years, you will find that the womb-to-tomb or womb-to-wedding book is almost extinct.

We have stressed the words "structure" and "chronological." Life-story novels are still valid and popular when constructed around an original framework. In *Portnoy's Complaint,* the past action of the book, really the entire story, is almost chronological. But the present action, taking place in a psychiatrist's office, gives it a contemporary structure—or at least a contemporary disguise. A less successful novel, James Baldwin's *Tell Me How Long the Train's Been Gone,* is another chronological life-story. But Baldwin endowed it with a modern structure by using flashbacks, recollections of the leading character when he is stricken by a heart attack.

Novels, both old and new, are about human lives, and most good works of fiction reveal almost complete life-stories of several characters. But the modern novelist tends to show the past within the frame of some present conflict or crisis.

Despite this obvious change in fiction, many first novelists produce rewrites of James T. Farrell, Vardis Fisher, and Thomas Wolfe—chronological life-stories based in varying degrees on their own lives. I have seen more than a score of unpublished (and quite unpublishable) novels, all of which, with changes of sex, time, and location, conform to the following outdated synopsis:

"Part One tells of John's childhood—his over-protective mother and brutal father. We meet John's brothers and sisters. There is also a kindly teacher who instills a love of books and poetry in John . . . Part Two is about high school and college days, his callow attempts at lovemaking and his adolescent sufferings . . . Part Three finds John in the army and reveals his shock at the horrors of combat . . . Part Four tells how he finds real love and consolation in the arms of a lovely girl who teaches him that beauty can be discovered even in ugliness."

This flat life-story might become a masterpiece in the hands of a genius—but I doubt that a genius would bother with it. It is *not* really a synopsis of a novel, but a description of a literary ego-trip, commonplace and unoriginal. There is no indication that the author has the faintest glimmer of the elements that make a novel: theme, issues, and ideas. His all-consuming interest is in telling a life-story, doubtless his own, in fictional form.

We must all face the fact that nobody, except perhaps the Credit Bureau, cares about the year by year history of our lives. Few of us have escaped from Devil's Island, scaled Mount Everest with a broken leg, or penetrated the Kremlin for the C.I.A. And if one has done any of those things, why write fiction? *The Reader's Digest* is panting for the true story.

A generation ago many chronological life-stories were successful novels of social protest. One thinks of Richard Wright's *Black Boy*. No doubt this type of life-story still has some potential for success. But such books are quite special. They do not chronicle the commonplace hopes and sufferings of an ordinary life against an ordinary background. And, alas, most life-stories penned by beginners do not include the unusual settings or powerful themes that would strengthen them.

Dr. Zhivago is indeed a life-story of its title character, and apparently many incidents and episodes are partly autobiographical. The author identifies himself with the doctor in many ways. But Boris Pasternak was too great an artist to let self-identification shrink his book. The novel is not merely a life-story, but a work rich in history, philosophy, and sheer poetry. Even so, its structure is a throwback to another era, and a modern writer who imitates it will be handicapped.

Despite all the problems involved in writing the story of one's own life (or some version of it), many new authors feel positively compelled to produce such works. The events of their lives are inside them screaming and hammering to get out like a child locked in a closet. They can produce nothing else until this task is done; they must have the release of revealing themselves on paper.

There is nothing shameful about this, and such a writer must do the job at once. He will learn much from the experience, he will acquire discipline, and will be working with words and narrative. Above all, it keeps him *writing*. But if the project is not to fail, he should keep several important things in mind:

1. Try to avoid straight year-by-year chronology. It is out of literary favor. Also, it takes great skill to make such

a narrative suspenseful. A more modern construction deals with a present crisis—a criminal trial, a divorce, a death—and the past is probed from a present-time viewpoint.

2. Avoid self-pity. Emerson wrote that "Literature is man's attempt to indemnify himself for the wrongs of his condition." If you, in fictional disguise, are your own chief character, be careful not to indemnify yourself on every page. Heroes in autobiographical novels tend to be hypersensitive, overly misunderstood, and much too long-suffering. The writer must try to see himself with detachment—and this is not easy. There is a constant temptation to write a three-hundred page lament called, "Nobody Knows the Troubles I've Seen."

3. Recognize that the events of your life, so important to you, are of little interest to the world in general. Who cares if you had a drunken father? He means nothing to the reader until he is so vividly portrayed that one can smell the gin on his breath. The fact that every event you tell actually took place in life is of no help at all.

4. A life-story, whether of your own life or another's, is nevertheless a novel, and must behave as one. A chain of events or years is not enough. There must be a theme, a central idea which controls the incidents. What does the action *mean?*

5. Do your best and hope for the best, but do not expect too much from this novel. You may fall in love with your own life-story. Criticisms of it will be as painful as St. Sebastian's arrows, and its rejection can feel like the rejection of one's whole being. Guard against this from the start, and force yourself to look upon this work with the same objectivity you apply to anything else you write. Even if the work does not succeed financially, do not re-

gard it as a failure. You will have learned from the writing. And you will have got something out of your system, thus freeing yourself for other creations.

Life-story short story

All the foregoing has been about novels. Strange as it seems, most of the difficulties mentioned above do not apply to the autobiographical short story. Much of the best fiction written by novices is based on lived experience, and the same author who fails in a biographical novel may write a beautiful piece about some single experience in his own life.

I do not know all the reasons why this should be true— but true it is. Perhaps a writer can more easily find meaning in a single event or situation from his past, while the overall themes of his life remain confusing and elusive.

At any rate, your past contains a wealth of raw material for potential short stories. But emphasis is on the word "raw," and for once in reference to modern fiction "raw" does not mean salacious but undeveloped. Real events almost always require forming and shaping to turn them into fiction.

Some true incidents can be transformed into stories with comparatively little difficulty; others are harder to develop, and some prove to be impossible—blind alleys that at first glance seemed to be passageways. There are many factors that determine what is usable for fiction and what is not, but I would like to concentrate on one of the most important—the question of *meaning*.

Almost everyone remembers a perennial school writing assignment that always came in September: "How I Spent My Summer Vacation." This task in composition elicited a good deal of information from the pupil and the results were narratives, however formless. The fiction writer who proposes to use real happenings as a basis for a story is in effect re-doing this fifth grade essay, but with a more sophisticated title: "What My Summer Vacation Meant to Me."

The difference between these two titles is vital and goes to the very heart of fiction writing. *What it meant . . .*

If John Smith is chased by a tiger, the event will be exciting only insofar as it means something to John himself —or perhaps to his horrified wife who is watching the race. *Meaning* is obviously connected with *feeling,* and both are indispensable to good fiction, but I am stressing the former here because it is in this area that so many writers come to grief when they translate real incidents into fiction.

Let us say that you were unlucky enough to be mugged on a dark street last winter. That, surely, is a dramatic event and might become a terrifying short story. But before you spend time writing this tale, I suggest you consider carefully what it all meant to you. Did it in any way change your life? Your philosophy? Were you exactly the same person when you left that dark street as when you entered it? If the experience had no meaning to you apart from temporary fright and unpleasantness and you cannot find an imagined meaning, then I suspect you will waste your time writing this story. (Unless you treat it as a grim comedy or tack on an O. Henry twist revealing that you yourself are a professional mugger. And pure "twists" fare badly in modern fiction.)

The writer's constant search to find meaning in events is by no means confined to stories based on life. It is a major factor in all good fiction. But we raise the subject here because the meaning of a real event is so often the reef upon which an otherwise promising story founders. A young writer vividly recalls an experience which moved him profoundly, and it can be anything from the death of a pet dog to a campus riot. Because he is writing about a deeply felt happening, the muse is on his side. His honest emotion carries us along through a series of events as he tells a moving story. Then, almost at the end, everything collapses. His well-told incidents prove meaningless and therefore pointless and disconnected. We may have had a good journey, but if the final destination was nowhere, we are left annoyed and unsatisfied.

Modern readers are more inclined to accept "journeys to nowhere" than their fathers were. But a story that is a bit weak in theme and meaning must be exceptionally good in every other regard, or it all adds up to nothing.

In essence, everything comes back to the matter of "How I Spent My Summer Vacation" as against "What My Summer Vacation Meant to Me." A wise writer will quickly learn that the second title is the gauge by which he measures the possibilities of potential story material. The first title will remain what it always has been, a grammar school essay—and not a very promising one.

~ 4 ~

GAMES WRITERS PLAY

WRITING has often been described as being less a profession than a "way of life." I am not entirely sure what that statement means, but I do know that the fiction writer's work is never done.

Even though he has completed his scheduled hours of labor and is trying to thrust his current story from his mind, the task continues—often subconsciously. A fiction writer is a perpetual hunter, a scout on the lookout for characters, ideas, remarks and situations that may later be shaped and molded to become part of his work.

Most of this foraging is not done with premeditation. Good writers are by nature listeners and observers. A sharp eye, a keen ear, a sense of undercurrents and overtones are a part of talent. Fortunately this is one aspect of talent that can be cultivated. A writer, through self-discipline, is able to improve his habits of observation.

Certain events in life are so obvious and memorable that we hardly need comment on them. Anyone who has felt the ground shudder beneath him in an earthquake or

seen a great tree split by a lightning bolt is likely to notice and remember. On a less dramatic level, we all meet
people who are so outrageous or beautiful or ugly that
their characteristics impress us. We are also likely to take
note of an especially witty or pungent remark someone
has made. All this is natural and easy. The more difficult
task and the skill a writer should develop is the ability to
notice and remember things less memorable in both his
outer and inner worlds.

Practical observation, done consciously, is not only invaluable, but it is one of the few jobs in writing that offers
pleasure without hard work. I find it a fascinating game,
rewarding both personally and literarily. Deliberate attempts to see, hear, and feel as a writer have rescued me
from boredom and have even helped me get through situations filled with stress and grief.

There is an area of my life which I call the Department of Useless Experience. Utterly boring but quite in-
escapable situations are found in this sector: dreary cocktail parties I've been roped into; long trips through
familiar and uninteresting country; pointless lectures de-
livered in monotone; waiting forever in any kind of
office; a weekend at a resort where it rains unceas-
ingly . . .

We all find ourselves in such entrapments, caught in
the Department of Useless Experience. Under such circumstances, I try to protect my sanity and hopefully to
render the useless usable by becoming "A Writer" and
playing a game of literary observation.

For example, let's consider that social torture, the boring cocktail party. There are too many guests with too
little in common, talk is on the shallowest level of chit-
chat, and every smile in the room is a practiced exercise.
That is the time when I *really* start listening and watch-

ing. "What can these people give me?" I ask myself. Under the circumstances, one can hardly expect to hear anything witty or profound, so I listen for banalities. Can I collect six classic clichés to sum up all the conversation around me? Who is the worst bore present, and exactly why is he so boring? How could I catch his character on paper—convey his boring talk without putting a reader to sleep?

What about the "stage properties"? Is there something on the mantel that reveals the personality of the host? Do the pictures on the walls (or the lack of pictures) tell me anything? Could they be intended to deceive me?

Turning from the real situation around me, I unleash my imagination, using the classic fiction writer's "What if—?"

What if someone slipped LSD into the martini pitcher? What particular hallucinations would these guests suffer or enjoy? Or maybe someone poisons Mrs. Smith's rum collins. Who? Why? How? Can I think of an opening sentence for such a story?

The people around me seem ordinary, pedestrian. Do they have secret lives? Hidden passions and hatreds? The tortured, twisted characters in Sherwood Anderson's *Winesburg, Ohio* must have appeared ordinary and even dull on the surface. But their inner lives were strange, beautiful, and often terrifying. Is it the same in this room?

Such exercises in observation, done consciously and as a means of self-defense, have yielded me a wealth of material. While waiting in an airport I noticed an elderly lady poring over a lurid true crime magazine, devouring its illustrated reports of mayhem and abduction. As I wondered how I might describe this woman in fiction, it struck me that her dark dress and some aspects of her face reminded me—of all things—of the famous portrait of Whistler's mother. Whistler's mother and crimes of violence? I made a mental note and later a written one, "Whistler's mother, arch-criminal." About two weeks afterward I began the story, "Do Your Christmas Shoplifting Early," and its central character was indeed Mrs. Whistler. "Shoplifting" has been reprinted many times and I hereby gratefully dedicate it to the unknown woman in the airport.

My story, "Evening at the Black House," a very successful short story, would never have been written if I had not been playing the game of "What if—" on an occasion when a gossipy but uninteresting lady talked about the odd behavior of a German family who had a house near the village where I lived. I cannot recall exactly what the lady said. Her remarks struck me as pointless and trivial, but suddenly I realized that she was giving me the seed of a story when she remarked, "Those people could be fugitive Nazis for all anyone knows." My imagination started racing. This was only a seed—it would require a great deal of cultivating to turn it into effective fiction. But the game of listening and thinking "What if—" had again proved its value—this time the result was a story for *Cosmopolitan.*

Let me stress that this bit of gossip, no doubt false and malicious, was no more than a springboard for creativity. I had to play the entire game of "What if—" alone. What if the people mentioned *were* Nazi criminals in hiding? What would their lives be like? What would threaten them (conflict)? Who would tell the story (viewpoint)? What would the imagined events mean (theme)? What about character and atmosphere? These and other questions had to be worked out. But if I had not been *lis-*

tening as a fiction writer in the first place, the idea for the story would not have come to me.

There is another, rather different game of observation that I recommend. It might be called, "Giving yourself an assignment."

Several times each week necessary errands make me walk several blocks through streets which have been familiar to me for years. The route is always the same; I think I could take this walk in pitch dark without stumbling. Unless my mind is completely occupied with other matters on a given day, I make a conscious effort to see something different, *to notice*. These blocks, although I know them so well, still contain infinite possibilities for fiction. I am seldom disappointed. The smile or frown of a passerby catches my attention for a moment; I glance at a broken shutter hanging by one hinge and somehow —I don't know why—it suggests loneliness. Last year, after such a walk, I jotted down, "Hummingbird among the blossoms of copa de Oro. Emerald on gold." This image, slightly expanded, is now being used in the second chapter of a novel I am currently working on.

I do not expect to find a polished story or a chapter of a novel lying in the street waiting to be picked up. Most of my observations, although interesting momentarily, will not be usable. But, after all, I am only hoping to catch one significant detail out of a thousand tries. One out of a thousand seems a very good batting average to me.

So far we have spoken only about observing the outer world. But the writer's inner world is at least equally important, and one must keep a sharp eye on it.

We all have periods of trouble and difficulty—times of pain, fear, and discomfort. A writer in such straits can put his troubles to work. He can say to himself quite deliberately and consciously, "How does this pain feel? How *exactly?* Could I express it on paper?"

Some time ago, a good friend of mine died. I found her loss hard to bear, and all consolations seemed futile and empty. It was a difficult time, and one thing that helped me through it was a conscious analysis of my own grief. I examined my loss not as a bereaved survivor, but as a writer viewing one of life's tragedies. Of what was my sadness compounded? How much of what I felt was self-pity? What were my physical reactions to this emotional shock? I wondered which concrete details would make my experience meaningful to a reader—for I had begun to realize that some day, in a fictionalized version, I would use some part of this tragedy. I did. Every emotion I felt then was later shared by the fictional characters in my novel *The Inquisitor's House.* During my time of mourning I wrote in a notebook: "Some men can drop a final bread crust into an open grave, hear the rattle of a handful of gravel on a coffin lid, then turn away forever. They can walk home, stumbling perhaps, their shoulders hunched by a burden of grief, yet they soon let go of what is left behind. They resume their day to day lives, eventually finding new love, new grief. But other men are not of this breed. . . ."

These words appear in *The Inquisitor's House,* unchanged except for the tense.

The game of self-observation with an eye to fictional results has stood me in good stead in many other troublesome situations. To mention just one: I have half a notebook filled with scrawlings made while I was in a hospital bed: "The hunchback orderly. Beautiful, sad eyes in a monkey's face. Wonderfully dexterous hands. He speaks as much with his hands as with his voice." This observation was the basis of the character "Little Brother" in *The Inquisitor's House*, and a true story told me by a fellow patient gave me the character Dolores Cortes in the same novel. Other notes made during that time of enforced leisure will undoubtedly find their places in my fiction in the future.

Every writer must develop his own method of viewing the world, his own "games." My rather systematic attempt will not work or be necessary for everyone. But I urge all beginners to give it a try. Observation done deliberately at first may later become an unconscious habit, and eventually the writer might be able to share the smugness of Sherlock Holmes who said, "It is my business to know things. Perhaps I have trained myself to see what others overlook."

Notebooks

The most brilliant observations of life are quite useless if the writer cannot remember them afterward. The standard solution to this difficulty is summed up in the classroom advice: "Keep a notebook faithfully. Record anything that may be of possible use later."

However, a great many fine fiction writers scoff at this, saying, "My notebook is in my head. If I can't remember something, it probably isn't worth remembering anyway."

Since my own wretched memory is helped by writing things down—even though I may never refer to the reminders afterward—I am squarely on the side of the notebook-keepers. Besides, empty notebooks present a challenge. I am more likely to be on the lookout for good ideas if I know I am going to write them down at once.

Again, the matter is personal, a question of finding one's own best way of working. Since this is the case, we will not spend much time on the notebook problem here.

However, my own experience (and the experience of other writers I know) leads me to believe that there are three definite rules about notebook-keeping that any writer would do well to follow:

1. Write down enough or don't bother at all. My early journals are filled with enigmatic fragments. For instance, I find, "The lady in the purple dress at A.P.'s house." When I jotted this down, it must have had some significance. Now I do not know for the life of me who "A.P." was, much less the lady. No amount of brain-racking brings the event back to me—and it is my loss. Why hadn't I sense enough to write a little more? Now I know better.

2. If you note words or ideas of other writers, put such things in quotation marks and name the source. I have a habit of entering bits of literature or thoughts that stimulate my mind. Years ago I was confident that I would always remember where such entries came from. In my early notebooks there are a number of good observations I dare not use, because I am no longer certain that they are my own. Some are in quotation marks, but since no author is credited, they might well be remarks made by an acquaintance. So these good, pithy sentences I thought worth recalling are now unusable.

3. Don't make notes in public. Nothing makes people freeze faster than the sight of something being written down. They are immediately on guard, their talk and behavior become unnatural. Besides, you might be mistaken for a spy. Or, worse yet, you might be thought a

writer. Some years ago I sat in a sidewalk café in Vera-
cruz, a notebook and pencil on the table before me. A be-
spectacled young man who I supposed was an American
entered, took a chair not far from me, drew a notebook
and pen from his pocket, and was soon intently watching
and making jottings about passersby. What, I wondered,
could I note about *him?* Well, the obvious thing was that
he was a writer or a would-be writer, and this show-off
performance was trumpeting the fact to all the world.
Did he secretly hope someone would ask him, so he could
reply with proper false modesty, "Yes, it just happens I
am an author. However did you guess?"

I felt my face reddening. As unobtrusively as possible I
put away my notebook—and I have never taken it out in
public since!

~ 5 ~

ANALYTICAL READING—FICTION
INSIDE OUT

IF a person has at least some talent, there are only two absolute requirements for acquiring the *craft*—if not the art—of fiction writing.

Instruction and editorial criticism can be most helpful and will certainly shorten one's apprenticeship. Certain writers need outside encouragement to keep going; and long, uninterrupted periods of time make a potential author's life easier. Desirable though these things are, they are not indispensable. A person with enough determination and talent may succeed without any such advantages.

But no one can produce effective fiction without fulfilling two basic prerequisites first:

1. He must write—perform the manual labor of putting words on paper. And probably he must write ten times as much as he first thinks is necessary.

2. He must read. And he must learn to read not as a layman but as a *writer*.

The first requirement is obvious and we will not stress

it further here. But the second, the matter of reading, is more complex.

Some authors seem born with a natural ability to read analytically, and I envy them. They unconsciously sense the rhythms and techniques of a story. Others must learn to read as writers.

When I first began to produce fiction, I had behind me years of experience in other types of writing. And all my life I had devoured novels and short stories. I flattered myself that I was "very widely read." Then to my amazement I discovered that I had never really read at all. Never had I unraveled a story to learn how it had been woven by the author. I had read critically, but not analytically, and there is a great difference. It is one thing to check the accuracy of a clock, and quite another to take it apart spring by spring. It is only by taking it apart that you will fully understand what makes it tick.

A friend of mine, a widely-published author and a prominent editor, told me how he wrote his first successful story, which was published by *The New Yorker.* "The magazine had rejected other things I'd written. Then I read one of their stories carefully. I reread it, looked at it paragraph by paragraph, and suddenly I saw how it was put together, how it 'worked' and developed. The story I later wrote was quite different, and was my own. But I know I couldn't have produced it if I hadn't studied the other writer's work."

In other words, analytical reading. He had discovered how certain effects were achieved.

How does one analyze a passage of fiction? As an example, here is the opening of Flannery O'Connor's excellent novel, *The Violent Bear It Away:*

Francis Marion Tarwater's uncle had been dead for only half a day when the boy got too drunk to finish digging his grave and a Negro named Buford Munson, who had come to get a jug filled, had to finish it and drag the body from the breakfast table where it was still sitting and bury it in a decent and Christian way, with the sign of its Savior at the head of the grave and enough dirt on top to keep the dogs from digging it up. Buford had come along about noon and when he left at sundown, the boy, Tarwater, had never returned from the still.

The old man had been Tarwater's great-uncle, or said he was, and they had always lived together so far as the child knew. His uncle had said he was seventy years of age at the time he had rescued and undertaken to bring him up; he was eighty-four when he died. Tarwater figured this made his own age fourteen. His uncle had taught him Figures, Reading, Writing, and History beginning with Adam expelled from the Garden and going on down through the presidents to Herbert Hoover and on in speculation toward the Second Coming and the Day of Judgment. Besides giving him a good education, he had rescued him from his only other connection, old Tarwater's nephew, a schoolteacher who had no child of his own at the time and wanted this one of his dead sister's to raise according to his own ideas. . . .

The first effect I feel in reading this passage is a sense of being plunged headlong into the story. No wasted time, no wasted words. In just two paragraphs, Miss O'Connor has brought us into her world and given us a surprising amount of information about both the boy Tarwater and his uncle. A writer's first question is: How did she do it? *Exactly* how?

Obviously the result came from the careful selection of details. The first three words, the boy's name, suggest the southern United States and, almost specifically, Georgia. Francis Marion was, of course, the famed "Georgia Swamp Fox" in the Revolutionary War, and "Tarwater" very subtly suggests "Tar Heel." We are shown backwoods isolation at once. There is only the boy and later Buford Munson to dig a grave.

Even a novice writer knows that one must "show things, not just tell them." This principle of good fiction strikes us as we examine the passage above. Miss O'Connor does not make a weak, general statement: "The old man was a Fundamentalist Protestant." Instead, she shows us his religion by revealing what he taught the boy, an angry faith that begins not with the creation of the world, but with punishment upon Adam. Nor does she say, "He was a moonshiner who operated a still." She shows it by action.

The writing is strong, authoritative. One reason, we discover by analysis, is that it contains not one descriptive adverb. (For those who wouldn't know a descriptive adverb if it modified them—and some excellent writers wouldn't—we'll simply say that a descriptive adverb usually ends in "ly.") We have all been warned against using too many adverbs, but when we see Flannery O'Connor's parsimony with them, the lesson becomes dramatic. (Georges Simenon, by the way, has said that when he pares his manuscripts and gives final polishing, the first thing he does is to delete almost every adverb.)

Why does Miss O'Connor need no adverbs? Because she has chosen the right verbs. Moral: if your manuscript is loaded with "lys," pruning half of them will help, but may not correct the real fault. Overuse of adverbs indicates poor, weak verbs. One sometimes writes "walked unsteadily" because the verbs "tottered" or "staggered" did not come to mind; "the mouse moved swiftly and suddenly" really means "the mouse darted." Adverb-studded writing is a warning to check your verbs for exactness.

Returning to our analysis, we note that a bit of suspense, a suggestion of future conflict has been neatly planted at the end of the second paragraph. A relative, a schoolteacher, is mentioned. We know that Tarwater has been "rescued" from him. Will the schoolteacher now play a role in the boy's future? We must read on to learn the answer.

Our analysis remains incomplete. What pattern of sentence structure has the author employed? How does she vary it? What is the effect of capitalizing such words as History and Figures? There is a score of things to be learned from these two paragraphs.

Some readers might not feel the power and strength I find in this passage. When that is the case the question becomes: How, exactly, did the author fail? What's wrong? How could it be corrected? We can learn much from writing we neither admire nor enjoy.

Analytical reading—reading as a writer—is the keystone of most valid systems of teaching writing. Authorities agree that a beginner should take the works of good authors and turn them inside out to study every seam and stitch. But an analysis need not follow the pattern I have set down. Different people will develop individual ways most useful to themselves. But whatever the method, the reading must be *detailed* and the observations *concrete* to be of value. General impressions and critical evaluations about the origin of a work will not help. A writer, when reading for professional education, is less interested in *what* another has done than *how* he did it—or exactly where he failed.

Naturally it would be time-consuming and hardly worthwhile to apply the method shown here to an entire novel. Such an analysis of *The Violent Bear It Away* would be at least three times as long as the book itself. But a potential novelist should certainly analyze many works chapter by chapter to inspect the understructure. What purpose does a certain section of dialogue serve? How does Chapter Six advance the plot? The theme? What are the *exact* functions of various characters?

One last word: I do not for a moment suggest that writers lose either their innocence or enthusiasm when reading as a *reader*. Starting to read a new novel or story should be an exciting experience, and one is not excited crawling down the margins, pencil in hand, notebook at elbow. When a writer encounters a new work, he reads it as anyone would.

But if he decides to reread for analysis, he becomes a different man—a dissector, an anatomist. By the time he has finished he will have learned things about his craft that he can discover in no other way.

~ 6 ~

DISCOVERING FICTIONAL CHARACTERS

SINCE stories are about people, the success of almost every work of fiction depends upon its characters. A plot may be weak, a theme banal, a background colorless, but if the characters in a narrative are fascinating and memorable, the work rises above almost all faults. Readers are more likely to tolerate an author's deficiencies as long as the characterizations are vivid and moving.

It has often been said (although less frequently in recent years) that in certain fields of writing, plot is the major factor and characters count for little. This remark usually is applied to detective stories, science fiction, and adventure tales. The belief that plot alone will carry a short story—much less a novel—is an outdated idea, and it was never the whole truth anyway.

In the detective field, for instance, the "pure puzzle" is seldom welcomed by publishers or readers. Even during the 1930s, the heyday of the mystery story, when people would read almost anything that involved murder and its detection, the most popular authors all had the gift of creating lively and entertaining characters. Agatha Christie's portraits of people may be superficial, but they are always deft and distinctive. Such authors as Georges Simenon and the late Josephine Tey have raised the standards of detective fiction immeasurably. Patricia Highsmith, Ross Macdonald, and Emma Lathen are among the detective fiction writers who have taught us that people are far more important than puzzles.

People are also more important than shipwrecks, typhoons, and spooky old houses. Mary Stewart, Victoria Holt, and Phyllis Whitney have given the antique romantic novel of suspense a new lease on life by creating exactly the right characters for their millions of readers to feel and believe in. All three of these writers are skillful plotters and create the sense of atmosphere their audience demands. But these talents would count for nothing if they lacked the ability to bring their fictional people onto the mysterious scene alive and developed.

John le Carré has revolutionized the espionage novel, and since the publication of *The Spy Who Came in from the Cold,* that field of writing has never been the same as it used to be. Eric Ambler's interest has also shifted over the years away from plots and toward persons. Characterization, always the prime ingredient of storytelling, dominates every type of fiction today.

A fictional character is seldom born complete. Usually he arrives in an author's mind piecemeal, as fragments in the imagination or memory: an odd face, a pair of gnarled hands, an ill-fitting overcoat—intriguing elements not yet attached to a whole body or identified with a personality.

But a character may start as a replica of a real person known to the author. In most cases, however, the resemblance to the life model diminishes as a story progresses.

The heroine who began as one's own Aunt Agatha in Chapter One has been transformed by Chapter Five.

It is well known that both Charlotte and Emily Brontë used their brother Branwell as a model for the heroes of their respective novels, *Jane Eyre* and *Wuthering Heights*. But Charlotte's fictional Mr. Rochester has only superficial similarities to Emily's Heathcliff, and neither character is a portrait of the Branwell Brontë biographers have revealed. Life models are transfigured by the demands of a story.

John Steinbeck is often mentioned as an author who used acquaintances for fictional purposes. This is to some extent true, but I myself knew many of the people who were fictionalized by Steinbeck, and the differences between the actual characters and the literary versions were just as striking as the many resemblances.

The way a character first comes to a writer is a personal, individual matter. Sometimes there is a life model. More often the character is a composite of several people —Aunt Agatha's appearance, Grandma's personality, and Cousin Mary's peculiar voice. Other authors invent from whole cloth; still others use historical models. Most writers, I believe, do all these things.

No one can give a writer much helpful advice about the *initial* inspiration for a character. Obviously it is best to write about people who arouse strong feelings of some sort in the author himself. It is also obvious that if a writer has a definite plot (a series of cause and effect actions) and a definite theme (a controlling idea) in mind, then the characters must be selected for the particular situation.

Since portraying a character is a highly personal matter, I must approach the subject through my own experience. There are certain routines I follow—some of them almost unconsciously—and to my surprise I have learned that many other writers do almost the same things—with variations, of course.

When I have an idea for a character, even if the idea is quite hazy, I immediately assume that that character is a real person. This is crucial! Since he already exists, my task is not to "create" him, but to discover his personality and features. I am not working as a sculptor, but as a detective. I must first make the acquaintance of this imaginary man, then get to know him well, and finally learn every hidden facet of his being.

Of course, I know perfectly well that the figure finally emerging in the story or novel will be my own invention, but I must not think of my fictional creation in this way during the process of planning or writing. The character, I repeat firmly, *exists*. He is real and whole from the beginning, and seems incomplete at first only because I have had no more than a fleeting glimpse of him.

This approach must not be dismissed as "merely a method of thinking." There is no "merely" about it! The author's attitude toward his characters is all-important. If he does not believe their reality, no one else will. Psychologically there is a vast difference between asking "What is John Jones like?" and "What shall I make John Jones?" The first question affirms the character's reality, his truth; the second suggests he is going to be something turned out in a welding shop. I, at least, cannot say to myself, "I'll give John Jones two teaspoons of courage, a pinch of kindness, and half a cup of intelligence." I want no recipes, no jigsaw puzzles that pieced together become a human figure. A pieced-together character is not real in the author's mind.

Avoiding false notes

The writer who firmly believes in the independent reality of his fictional people and who knows their natures well will instantly detect false notes and improbabilities of behavior. It is rather like the Stanislavsky Method of acting: If one knows the character, has utter belief in him, and almost *becomes* the character in imagination, then natural actions and reactions will result.

It is the same in fiction writing. A writer who fully knows the character of John Jones both intellectually and emotionally, who actually *feels* him, will have no trouble deciding what John does when a bomb explodes on his front porch in Chapter Six; or when John's wife deserts him for a rock musician in Chapter Ten. The author who respects John's independent existence is unlikely to force the helpless fictional being into behavior contrary to his nature.

On the other hand, the author who regards his characters as marionettes who respond automatically to string-pulls is performing his act on a tightrope. The performer will crash to earth the moment a reader says, "Do you mean to tell me that that flint-hearted snob John Jones let his daughter marry the office boy with no protest? And gave them half a million as a wedding present? I don't believe it!" (Neither did the author believe it, and therein lies the trouble.)

Sometimes plot and character clash head on and the resultant false note is thunderous. For reasons of plot an honest, kindly man tells a malicious lie; or a cold, puritanical girl flings herself into the arms of the village rake. Such things do happen in life, and the obvious explanation is that Mr. Upright was not as honest as everyone thought, and Miss Prim not so straitlaced. But this will seldom serve in fiction. The author is supposed to know far more about his characters than the neighbors knew about Mr. Upright and Miss Prim. Unless the author has given at least subtle clues to the eventual turpitude of Upright and Prim, the reader has been cheated. (Sudden uncharacteristic behavior in the middle of a novel or short story is not to be confused with the surprising but fully explained actions that provide a mainspring for many excellent works: Faulkner's "A Rose for Emily," Styron's *Confessions of Nat Turner,* Maugham's *Moon and Sixpence,* for example.)

When a writer suspects a false note, he must be ruthless about eliminating it—and no amount of revision is too great. Either the character is wrong or the action is wrong, and something must be changed. But an experienced writer will think carefully before plunging into alterations. For there is a third possibility: Maybe both character and action are true, but the motivation for the act is weak or missing. Perhaps Mr. Upright is really a man of integrity, but unbearable pressures—which we have not yet discovered—forced him to tell lies.

Then the question becomes: "Why would such a good man behave so badly? What, aside from a writer's whim, made him do it?"

This approach puts the false note to work, and it may open new channels of imagination.

"Getting to know you"

The skeleton of a fictional character has appeared in a shadowy corner of the room. We cannot yet see him clearly, but an author's ESP reveals a few things about the man: He is elderly, approaching retirement age, and a workman to judge by his rough hands and rather stooped shoulders. His name, which we learned on the fifth guess, is Sam Hughes; he is a husband and father, but we do not yet know how many children he has.

Our skeleton is now taking on some flesh and even a bit of clothing, for we suddenly notice that he wears a billed, cloth workingman's cap of a type common a generation ago. Since not many factory workers wear such caps nowadays, Sam must be rather old-fashioned.

Before we press this acquaintanceship further, one major question must be answered: Is Sam Hughes worth knowing? Is there any distinctive feature that sets him apart, makes him interesting? If he does not arrest the imagination and arouse the curiosity, then it is better to forget him at once. Now is the time to think carefully.

At last the answer comes. Yes, his square jaw and rugged face reveal a man who is strong, stubborn, and determined. Yet there is a bewildered expression in his eyes. Does this tie in with the old-fashioned cap? Is Hughes a man baffled by the modern world, resentful and confused by changes he cannot accept or understand? This suggests a conflict. What if Sam Hughes has a son or daughter who has taken to drugs and is living in a hippie commune?

Suddenly we remember a newspaper story of a year or so ago. An agonized father killed his own daughter because he thought her life so immoral that she would be better off dead. Could Sam do this? (Perhaps Sam appeared because the story lurked in the back of our mind.) It seems possible, since we now notice that he is wearing a small religious medal, and in his worn billfold is a snapshot of his daughter dressed in lacy white for her first communion, a lovely child whose wistful eyes are gravely innocent.

Sam Hughes has now become a man decidedly worth knowing better. Still we hesitate. A story or perhaps a novel can be fashioned from the conflict we have thought of. It has the potential of becoming a powerful and gripping work. But although we may understand Sam's passions intellectually, can we comprehend him *emotionally?* Do Sam and his possible story fall within the scope of our own experience? Do we really want to tell this story? Does it seem to be "friendly" material?

Certain writers could give an immediate answer. Others would debate the matter. Still others would have to try writing a few pages or even more before they could know.

The important point is this: If a character and his potential story do not strike sparks in the writer's imagination and sympathy, then the project should be forgotten. It is not for that particular writer at that particular time of his life. The best that can be done is to make an entry in a notebook. Later, if Sam comes back to haunt one, the question is open for reconsideration.

Character and action

Our interest in Sam Hughes quickened the moment conflict and action suggested themselves. This brings us to a major principle: *A fictional character* is *what he* does.

The author who keeps this in mind will avoid dull, expository writing. The principle is really an extension of the old and true commandment to writers: "Show, don't tell."

If we write, "Sam Hughes was a deeply religious man who loved his daughter," the reader will accept these two facts, but they will have no emotional meaning. Sam Hughes seen at the factory where he bores fellow workmen by displaying his daughter's picture and endlessly describing her first communion could be a vivid scene. We will know him only when we hear the words of his prayers and see his rough hands become gentle as they count the beads of a rosary. ("Hail, Mary, full of grace!

The Lord is with Thee . . ." The hands tighten convulsively. "Oh, Mother of God, help me! What am I to do? I've given my girl everything, I've tried, I've prayed. And now this! Help me, help me!")

It is easy to fill in a questionnaire about a fictional character. One can list his age, height, weight, hobbies, religion, politics, and so on endlessly. This may be helpful as a manner of organized thinking and an author should certainly know all these facts. But such a dossier, because it lacks action, will never capture the essence of personality.

We might say that Sam Hughes is a conservative Democrat. This information will help a poll-taker, but is not of much use to a writer. Does Sam glue political bumper-stickers on his car? What do they say? What does he do when the union steward passes the hat to support a political candidate? Does Sam attend rallies? The man can be portrayed only in action. (Speaking and thinking are also forms of action.)

When one first tries to discover a character, it is natural to use simple labels to sum up an impression: Sam Hughes is "patriotic," "not well educated," and "a loving but dominating parent." Handy, these labels. But a label is not the package itself! "Patriotic" is meaningless until the writer feels Sam's heart beat faster when a band plays "The Star-Spangled Banner," and hears Sam's infuriated reply to a "young punk" who calls the United States "Fascist Pig Amerika." Will Sam knock the blasphemer down? If the author does not know, he is not yet acquainted with Sam Hughes and not ready to write about him.

When a group of characters have all been well and truly discovered and the author's acquaintance with them has become deep and emotional, sometimes a startling thing happens. The characters seem literally to take over the writing; they begin to act on their own, to seize the author's story and run away with it. This is a glorious moment, an event for which writers pray.

I've heard many authors discuss this matter with something like awe in their voices. "I never expected them to do what they did!" It is hard to describe the sensation one feels at such a time. You seem to have ceased being a creator of anything. The fictional people have suddenly turned you into a stenographer or court reporter.

I suspect this has been the case when an author says, "Why, the book seemed to write itself!"

When this happens, it is time for the writer to get out of the way of the characters. Forget your well-planned plot, ignore your chapter-by-chapter outline! The fictional people have come to life, now let them live.

Later on, when revising, you may change many things that happened during this rebellion of characters. Maybe they abused their freedom. But editing and revising are colder tasks than actual writing, more intellectual and less emotional. At that point in your work you need not fear the disruption of feeling that may happen if you try too sternly to control a character who wants to break free.

But during the writing itself one must always remember that the characters *exist*. They are real people with their own personalities, and a wise author will respect their independence.

~ 7 ~

THE FULL-DIMENSIONAL CHARACTER

IN the midst of the struggle to write a longer work of fiction with fully developed characters, I find it necessary to get away from the typewriter and do some methodical thinking about the people I am trying to present to readers.

A writer, while working, is *always* thinking about his story and its people, but the kind of reflection I refer to here is a different matter. I mean time spent in considering the characters quite apart from plot or the problems of writing a certain passage. I do not mean the generalized mulling and pondering one does at idle moments. I speak of planned and organized meditation.

This meditation cannot be done until I am fairly well acquainted with the characters. I know a good many things about them, have seen them in action, and am aware of their quirks and foibles. One might call them "surface characters." Then comes the time to probe for depth, to do painstaking reconsideration. I must answer a long list of questions about these fictional people.

A character has certain dimensions—length, height, width—and these dimensions are on many planes. There are physical dimensions and psychological dimensions; a man's imagination has a certain scope and his station in life has sociological measurements. Moral and ethical values also have a given height or depth.

But human dimensions and values lie in the eye of the beholder. A tiny child might think his big sister enormously tall, while the girl's father could call her short, and she herself might say, "Average." A slum family could honestly describe their landlord as "a rich man," but the banker who holds the mortgage on the tenement would peg the owner as "lower middle class." Meanwhile, the landlord himself is in all sincerity bewailing his poverty.

Since dimensions are relative, I try to examine my fictional people from three distinct points of view. Sometimes the measurements and evaluations coincide; more often they do not. I am striving for a nebulous thing called "truth," and in the process I hope to deepen my acquaintance with my fictional men and women.

Here, in very abbreviated form, is an example of how this three-dimensional thinking process works:

In writing my novel *The Inquisitor's House*, I spent many hours struggling to know a character called Pierre Laurier, a man who seemed rather simple and shallow at first glance, but who was actually quite complex.

1. What do I myself think of Pierre Laurier? He's a swindler and a confidence man—conceited, cowardly, but gifted with surface charm. I do not find him physically attractive, but will admit he is handsome as Hollywood understood "handsome" a generation ago. He is worthless, yet I cannot help pitying him. I don't like him. Yet he might be amusing company under the right circumstances. Since he never really grew up, he has a child's cruelty. I'd like to call it "innocent cruelty," but I can't. He loves himself so much that he has no love left for anyone else. Perhaps this is why his life is empty and he is forever unsatisfied. He's quick-witted, but not really intelligent; has enough education to pass himself off as a "gentleman." His one constant loyalty is really an obsession, not a virtue. Underneath his braggadocio, he secretly hates himself and is bent on his own destruction.

2. How would Pierre Laurier describe himself? "I am a handsome devil and far cleverer than any man I have ever met. My luck is terrible, but despite my misfortunes, there's nothing on earth I couldn't do if I set my mind to it. Women find me irresistible, partly because of my good looks and partly because I am such a skillful lover. Women are useful to me, and I can always fascinate them. Some day I will do something great and the whole world will know my name and realize what a special person I am. Fate has made me do a few things I wouldn't have done otherwise, but I've never been unkind or dishonest unless I simply couldn't help it. An intelligent man like me has to make his way, and God created fools to help him do it. Success is just around the corner!"

3. What do the other characters in the book think of Pierre? The answer to this is too long and involved to be given here. But it is a question of great importance. The whole matter of relationships and conflicts in the novel comes to the fore at this point. As I delved into the opinions others held about Pierre, I had to change some of my own thinking. Pierre, I slowly realized, was sharper and more attractive than I had first thought him to be. Some revisions of my writing were called for.

The reconsideration of a fictional character I have given here is very condensed. My reflections about Pierre, who is a secondary character in *The Inquisitor's House,* would have filled many pages.

In essence, this method of thinking involves three basic questions that can be asked about all characters except those whose appearance in a work is so brief that no real development is possible. The dimensions of the major figures are examined from three points of view:
1. What do I, the author, think of this person?
2. What does he think of himself?
3. What do the other characters think of him?

Obviously there are moral and ethical judgments arising in all these questions. This is inevitable. Modern fiction is less moralistic than older works only in a superficial sense. A Victorian novelist might cast stones at a girl for pre-marital sex relations; a present-day writer of the new counter-culture may censure the same girl for feeling guilt after "a natural and beautiful love experience." The only difference is that the stones are hurled from the opposite direction.

This approach to knowing the people of a story is rendered worthless if the writer does not fully believe that his characters are real personalities capable of independent thought and action. During the course of writing *The Inquisitor's House,* I gradually acquired the feeling that the people of the novel were living with me. Although I certainly had no delusion of being "haunted," they followed me everywhere. They were driven, tormented people; one was a monster, and I detested several others. Not easy guests to have in the house! By the time the novel was finished these characters had so exhausted me emotionally that I had to take a "vacation" by writing a nonfiction book!

But I had to live with them and see each one through other eyes than my own. The writer who says "The characters in my book will think what I tell them to think about Mr. Jones" is setting up a psychological block, a barrier to imagination, invention, and creativity. His characters will not live for readers, because they did not live for the writer himself.

"Irrelevant Questions"

Once a character has been established to some degree and I have learned the main facets of his background and personality, I indulge in some mental gymnastics—a sort of game of the imagination which might be called "Irrelevant Questions." It is a practical exercise and one that deepens my knowledge of the fictional figure I am trying to portray.

I have described this as a "game" and I mean exactly that. It is not to be used as an excuse for taking time away from the actual labor of writing. One should not expect profound results. Nevertheless, I find it helpful. It works, and it works this way:

First, I invent a series of situations that demand reactions. They are *not* circumstances which will arise in the work I am writing at the time. In fact, I prefer them to be quite far removed, even farfetched.

Let's say we're wrestling with a character named George Jackson, and George is proving to be an elusive fellow to write about, indefinite and hard to comprehend.

Situation: George unexpectedly wins $50,000 in a sweepstakes. How, exactly, will he spend it? Equally important, how will he feel about spending it? Will he begrudge or enjoy every dollar? Now let's make his winnings $500,000. How will George's mode of living change? Will his politics shift? Will his behavior become overbearing and patronizing to old friends?

This imaginary situation will not teach us much about George if the man is already a multi-millionaire or if our story involves George's struggles to escape crushing debts. We require less relevant circumstances because we want to learn things that might not (we think) come up in the actual writing. We are hoping that "irrelevancies" of character will lead to practical discoveries.

Situation: George Jackson was aboard the *Andrea Doria* when it hit the *Stockholm* and sank. How did he behave? Did he knock down two old ladies and one small child in order to be first in a lifeboat? Or was he a hero? Or merely dazed? If dazed, what exactly did he do while in shock? Assuming he survived the shipwreck, how did he describe his own actions afterwards? Maybe he exaggerated his heroics and told bald lies. On the other hand, he might have been modest. Find the exact answers and you will have deepened your understanding of this man.

Situation: George Jackson goes to the zoo. Which animals attract him and which repel him? Why? If, for example, he finds a ring-tailed baboon especially repulsive, there must be a reason. Does it remind him of someone? Or arouse unpleasant memories of some childhood experience? The zoo experience is one of the best I know. Not only can it stimulate the imagination to new discoveries, but a whole symbolism for a character may suddenly emerge. Perhaps George is fascinated by a peacock because he is a peacock himself. New verbs occur to us: George preens and struts. We had not realized until now that George's eyes are glittering but empty, and his male beauty is actually all feathers but little muscle.

The zoo situation suggests a method of thinking used

by some actors in creating roles. They call it "finding the spine of the character," the word "spine" meaning a rather obvious symbol that sums up a personality. Human beings are enormously complex, and reducing a fictional character to a symbol often helps a writer get an initial hold. Naturally, the character will be developed far past a single symbol—George Jackson will become more than a peacock. But if we have grasped just one facet of George and found a way to express it, our time in the imaginary zoo has been well-spent.

To refer again to *The Inquisitor's House,* one repulsive character, a Spanish count, caused me trouble in writing until I realized the fascination this man would feel while watching a pit of serpents. From that moment on the character began to bask and coil, his eyes were hooded but curiously unblinking, he slithered, and he struck from ambush with deadly venom. After this side trip to a snake pit, I had no further unusual difficulty in handling the character.

Our game of "Irrelevant Questions" has in every case involved a person in a situation requiring definite action or reaction. Knowing what George Jackson did and felt during a disaster at sea is far more helpful than saying "George is brave" or "George is cowardly." It comes back to the fact that a fictional character *is* what he *does.* I find "Irrelevant Questions" a very relevant way of learning what actions result from definite circumstances.

One word of warning, however. If you put George into a whole series of situations, and each time a dozen conflicting courses of action suggest themselves but none seems more valid than another, then George Jackson is not a real man. Or at least he is not a man known to you. Speaking from sad experience and after much wasted effort, I suggest that George Jackson, after a reasonable amount of struggle, be forgotten altogether. Some characters simply refuse to gel, and when that happens one must remember that George is not the only man in the world. Better spend the time on Tom, Harry, or Dick whose reactions are more predictable and whose emotions you can share.

~ 8 ~

INTRODUCING A CHARACTER

YOU have discovered a fictional character—touched him, heard him, seen him, and shared his emotions. You still have much to learn about this man, but you know him well enough to begin writing. The task now is to introduce him to others.

At this point many novice writers become paralyzed by doubt. How much physical description should be given? How many details and which ones? And how quickly?

Often these problems, which are really not so difficult, appear insurmountable when one is sitting at a typewriter and the time has come to bring the fictional John Jones onto the scene. But everything becomes easier if one keeps a rather simple principle in mind: In modern fiction, a reader usually meets a fictional character in much the same way he encounters a person in life.

The majority of good contemporary authors introduce their characters in this natural fashion, and all beginners should. It is not a very daring or experimental method,

but it is safe and sound. Later on, after the apprenticeship is over, there will be time for a writer to indulge in
adventures and literary oddities.

Let us translate the principle into concrete events.
Suppose someone knocks at your door. The caller proves
to be a man taking an opinion poll for some organization,
and since he did not interrupt your writing schedule, you
do not set the watchdog on him, but take the time to answer his long list of questions.

You will have formed a general impression of this poll-
taker almost instantly. If he is a giant or a midget, the
fact has registered on you in the first second. Initial impressions are almost always visual. (Unless the caller
shouts "Anybody home?" before you see him, and even
then you will have no individualized impression unless
the voice is very distinctive.) This is supposedly the era of
unisex, but nevertheless one determines at once whether
the person is a man or woman. And a newcomer is
quickly assigned to some age group, especially if he is
very old or very young.

As the interview continues, certain details you did not
notice at first come to your attention: a slight tic under
the man's left eye, a trace of Texas in his speech, high
cheekbones. Very probably you will modify some of your
original impressions. You had thought at first that he was
ugly, but now you realize that he has a winning smile.
Perhaps you thought him so unattractive because of the
ill-fitting, drab suit he wears. Your impressions thus
slowly accumulate by a process of addition and correc-
tion.

In fiction as in life, this is the usual process of getting
acquainted. Most authors quickly give some brief physical description. Included in this is any feature that is especially striking—an eye-patch, a missing arm or leg, a

grotesquely large head, or some wild extreme of clothing. In other words, those things you would instantly observe in life. Other details that contribute to the portrait will come a little later, blended with dialogue and action— again, as in life.

This, in general, is the technique used by such authors as Philip Roth, John Cheever, John Updike, Graham Greene, Muriel Spark, and William Styron. Of course all of them vary their methods of presenting a character. Sometimes we are given many physical details and sometimes only a few. But there is a discernible pattern, and the apprentice writer would do well to study it carefully.

Is this method new? Peculiarly "modern?" The answer is a modified "no." The "as in life" introduction has been employed by authors in all centuries. However, the contemporary technique differs from certain ·approaches often used by other generations of writers.

Charles Dickens and Thomas Hardy often give us lengthy and highly detailed physical descriptions of major characters at the moment of introduction. Almost everything comes at once. They are wonderful portraits, but a modern reader is inclined to feel that Hardy, for example, is "taking time out" to present Eustacia Vye in *The Return of the Native.* In many Victorian novels, action halts while we read a descriptive essay, a head-to-heels physical examination—often with a microscope.

In the early part of this century, some authors rebelled and went to the opposite extreme, refusing to describe their characters at all or giving an absolute minimum of detail. We find this in Hemingway's first stories and in the more experimental works of Virginia Woolf.

The modern way, although it varies with individual authors, is a sensible compromise. We are told enough facts to identify a character physically, but are seldom asked to pause for a prolonged examination of an elaborate word portrait.

Many beginners seem unaware that the "never describe physically" method of writing fiction was always experimental and has been out of date for many years. Modern authors *do* describe their characters and often in great detail. But they do it more subtly and succinctly than their Victorian predecessors did, and will seldom spend time, for instance, cataloguing six facts about the eyebrow. And in many ways the contemporary author is more sensible than many popular writers of a generation ago. If the color of someone's eyes does not matter at all, except perhaps to heighten the illusion of reality, then there is little point in bringing up the fact. Stories found in popular magazines of the 1930s are often full of unnecessary information about a nose, chin, or hair style. They are not so extreme as Victorian examples, of course, but few writers of today would bother to note that "Mildred's hair was dull brown," if it has no bearing at all on her character or the story.

Nevertheless, physical description *is* used in modern fiction. The writer who capriciously refuses to reveal the height or coloring of his characters because of "artistic principles" not only indulges in silly affectation, but is living back in the 1920s.

The generation lapse

Let me tell you about my friend Mary Perkins. She's an adventurous type, and only last week she put on the most provocative hot pants she could find, donned an almost transparent blouse, and sprayed herself with a perfume reputed to turn men into beasts. Then she went hitchhiking. During the next hours, Mary accepted rides from seven different men, including three lonely truck drivers. Although she has beautiful eyes, a lovely smile, and was once runner-up in a major beauty contest, nothing happened to her that day. Absolutely nothing! Mary now swears that the Kinsey Report was an absurd exaggeration, and American men need psychiatric treatment or hormone shots.

Oh, by the way, I forgot to mention something. My friend Mary Perkins is ninety-seven years old. Looks every day of it, too, poor thing!

The "forgotten fact" casts a rather different light on the events of the story. I admit this is an extreme example, but I have seen otherwise well-written stories in which things only a little less preposterous escaped the author's attention. I do not refer to dreadful "surprise endings" where an essential bit of information is intentionally withheld.

It is imperative that the reader have some idea of an important character's age quite early in a narrative. Almost every interpretation is based to some extent on the age factor. For instance:

"I shall never marry until I meet the ideal man," said Linda.

If Linda is twelve years old, the remark shows natural naïveté. Add a few years to her age and the words become foolish romanticism. If Linda is over thirty, she must be rationalizing. It will not do for a writer to let this question hang in the air for a few pages until he gets around to telling us more about Linda. The effect originally intended will be lost by then.

Not long ago I read an interesting manuscript, a rather long story about a woman's disillusionment with love and sex. No specific age was assigned to the heroine, but judging from attitudes, actions and the reactions of others to her, I developed a mental picture of the girl. About twenty, I assumed, and a bit naïve for a young woman of today. Not very attractive physically, for men seemed to take her for granted. A handsome young lifeguard at a beach indicated a certain sexual interest in her, but his feelings were mild. As I read on, the picture grew more definite. I felt I knew her and I witnessed her experiences.

Then, about a page before the end, I discovered to my shock that this "girl" had a sixteen-year-old daughter! Blinking, I put down the manuscript and made a calculation. Age thirty-five? Maybe over forty! This heroine was not naïve—she was downright retarded. Every impression I had formed was mistaken. Since the lifeguard was almost a generation younger than this woman, she could not be as plain as I had supposed. Older but attractive. Or could the lifeguard be a gigolo? Or had the woman imagined his interest—wishful thinking? In order to make sense out of this story, I would have to reread the entire thing, and it would have lost the gloss of newness. Was it worth the effort? I thought not. Besides, I was irritated. Any reader would be.

The unexpected appearance of the daughter which revealed mama's age was not an intentional trick played by the author—thank God! The confusion arose because of stinginess in giving simple facts. If a reader has a chance to go astray, *he will!*

The threadbare mirror

Having a character look at himself in a mirror and then describe what he sees is such a convenient way of giving both a physical portrait and some emotional reactions that writers have employed it from time immemorial.

Since I recall using this device myself at least three

times, I feel sheepish about objecting to it. I am also aware that I may be reduced to using the mirror bit again. I hope to avoid it. I may not always be able to resist the temptation, however.

A long paragraph beginning, "Amanda gazed into the looking glass and frowned at her own features . . ." is undeniably cliché. Perhaps one can plead the excuse of reality. After all, people *do* consult their mirrors all the time and have reactions to what they see. There are few fiction writers living or dead who at one time or another have not resorted to this trite but very convenient device, so we may rationalize by saying, "Good enough for great masters, good enough for me."

But authors who send their protagonists to the mirror should be aware that they are less than original, and it is a good technique, but lackluster. Nevertheless, at this very moment some excellent author is writing the words "the mirror told her that she was . . ." And he will get away with it.

Too many trumpets

Often a character is introduced long before he actually appears in a story. Others talk about him, making such remarks as, "Just wait 'til you meet George! He's the handsomest man alive!" Later someone adds that George is irresistible, and some woman chimes in that it is because of his classic profile. At last George himself enters the scene, and the other characters, predictably, swoon.

This is an effective technique, not only for giving a description of George, but creating an "impending event" to build suspense.

Still, the method has its pitfalls. It's quite safe to say certain things about a character in advance, but extremely dangerous to talk about some other qualities.

A writer may herald George's physical and moral qualities, and may have someone tell George's life story without much risk. But an author who keeps trumpeting that George is witty, hilarious, and gifted with a side-splitting sense of humor and repartee is riding for a fall. To say that "George will keep you laughing all the time" is a challenge to the reader. When George appears, he must live up to the advance advertising, and a certain prejudice has been formed against him. "So he's going to be funny, is he? Well, you'll have to show me!"

It is equally hazardous to assure everyone in advance that George is gifted with amazing philosophical insight and depth. Again, the "show me" suspicion has been aroused, and the reader will be watching for George to show the least sign of shallowness or banality.

It will be noted that the hazard of the overbuilt entrance applies chiefly to mental traits of a character. Physical details are safe because, after all, the reader only imagines George and never sees him in the flesh. He must take the author's word that George is handsome. But the department of wit and wisdom is open for complete inspection. A reader judges these qualities by what George actually says—and he does not want the author's judgment thrust upon him.

What did he wear?

Clothes may not make the man, but they certainly reveal him. The garments designed to hide our naked bodies often expose our personalities in the raw. Being subject to colds and sunburns, I have little experience of nudist colonies. However, I am convinced that if I spent two hours with forty naked people, I would know less about them than if I saw the same group dressed in what they considered their best.

Philosopher-psychologist William James found clothes so intrinsic to character that he ranked a man's clothing as part of his very self. Of course, some people are highly conscious of their attire while others seem indifferent. Nevertheless, as James points out, some people will respond to an attack upon their clothing as they would react to a physical assault.

Clothing can be memorable. In my mind I never picture Sherlock Holmes bareheaded, and when someone mentions *The Catcher in the Rye,* the first thing I visualize is Holden Caulfield's ridiculous cap.

Since describing a significant article of attire is such a convenient method of introducing a character and tagging him for the reader, it has an inherent danger: overuse. Many hacks who churn out books and stories at breakneck speed fall back upon a monotonous and predictable formula. On page one you read: "Barbara Henderson, a statuesque girl in a strapless cocktail dress, came into the room." Then, a page later: "Old Mrs. Henderson, dressed in a lacy outfit much too young for her, descended the stairs." And then: "Mr. Henderson, a heavy-set man who wore country tweeds with elbow patches, joined the group."

Such a pattern glares like a neon sign announcing cheap craftsmanship. It reminds one of a description of a wedding party on a small-town society page. And aside from the monotony of repetition, only the youthful dress on old Mrs. Henderson really contributes to a character. "A strapless cocktail dress" is so general that, although we get some sort of picture, it in no way defines Barbara. Was it expensive or cheap? Flashy or plain? Modest or blatantly revealing? Any of these facts tells us more than "strapless." Mr. Henderson's tweeds and patches are better. The picture is fairly definite. But if it is worthwhile describing his clothes at all, then it is worth adding "well-worn" or "ill-fitting" or "elaborately casual" or any other term to show Henderson's character.

Although hand props—things people habitually carry and use—are not precisely clothing, they are at least accessories to costume, and in fiction they are highly effective in identifying a character and setting him apart. Certain fictional people are inseparable from various objects: Long John Silver and a parrot; Captain Queeg and his silvery ball bearings; Sarah Gamp and an umbrella; Madame Defarge and her knitting.

Such objects can be used to vary the "clothing pattern" and they quickly mark a character so the reader can identify him. An honorary sheriff's badge, an ostrich fan, an ivory toothpick, a hamster poking its head from someone's coat pocket . . . There are thousands of things ranging from the usual to the utterly bizarre that can lend a character distinction.

But if hand props are really unusual—like the hamster mentioned above—a very few will be enough for a book-length work unless the broadest comedy is intended.

My own resolutions in the matter of clothing and accessories for introducing characters boil down to three general principles:

1. Always be aware of the importance of clothing in revealing personality, but avoid any pattern in presenting it.

2. Never describe clothing just for its own sake, and be cautious about describing it to give a generalized picture. Tell what a character wears when the facts are meaningful and relevant.

3. Extreme accessories are effective, but use them sparingly, remembering that too many strong spices can spoil a dinner—or a story.

When not to characterize

Certain human figures who are not really characters at all often appear in fiction, such as, the waiter who brings drinks, the cab driver, the messenger boy, and many others. They have no real function in the dramatic or psychological action of the story itself. Should such people be characterized? Described? Made individual?

In general, the modern answer is no. Whenever such a figure is clearly portrayed—made individual—a reader expects him to do a good deal more than his role permits.

A waiter is a good case in point. If a scene takes place in an ordinary restaurant and its interest centers around a conversation at a certain table, then it is a mistake to write: "The waiter, a large man, slightly stoop-shouldered, brought martinis." If this man has nothing more to do, the description is merely slowing the action, cluttering the scene. Worse, it may lay a false trail for readers who will now expect the waiter's size to have some bearing on subsequent developments. "The waiter brought martinis" is far better.

There are two good reasons for making exceptions to the general rule. A completely incidental figure is often briefly characterized because the writer wishes to:

1. Reveal and intensify atmosphere or mood.

2. Create a foil for a more important character or show a facet of his personality.

One might write: "A beefy waiter with dirt-rimmed fingernails sullenly brought martinis." The purpose could be to show the atmosphere of a waterfront gin mill or some other dubious tavern. This is valid and effective. Further, it goes along with our "as in life" principle. We are quite likely to notice and remember a waiter whose appearance sums up the qualities of a certain place: the officious snob who condescends to serve us *haute cuisine* in an overpriced tourist trap, or the genteel lady who pours our tea in a "shoppe."

The sweltering heat of a tropical afternoon might be shown by a waiter who "shuffled and yawned." And we might speak volumes about the mood of an heroic nation at war if a waiter serves calmly and with an air of great elegance during an air raid.

It is also valid to make a waiter "groveling" or "fawning" to show the importance of the person being served. And incidental figures can point up ironies: A man and his wife are seated at a table. He says, "Darling, you must stop being jealous. I love only you! I wouldn't look at another woman!" Meanwhile, his wandering eye is inspecting the spectacular legs of the cocktail waitress. In this case, the provocative waitress becomes a foil, a method of revealing the man's insincerity.

There is yet a third reason for describing a walk-on character, but it is so subject to abuse that I hesitate to mention it: A writer has something so clever or original to say that he can't resist saying it. If it is really good and can't be reserved for a more important character, then by all means it should be included. Good judgment, tempered by moderation, is the only guide in such cases. But be careful. Does the cleverness really compensate for the irrelevancy?

Modern authors tend to eschew the little "cameo" descriptions of unimportant characters that older generations indulged in. Cameos, both real and literary, are not as popular as they once were. A beautiful one is never out of fashion, of course, but avoid pinning cheap decorations on unimportant figures.

When one is tempted to create a portrait gallery filled with paintings of clerks, elevator operators, ushers, and newsboys who have no genuine function in action or atmosphere, it is well to remember the "as in life" principle. Do we want to take the time to be introduced to people who will have no effect upon us and whom we shall never see again? Most of us don't. Not in life, and not in fiction.

~ 9 ~

BEWARE THE PAPER DRAGON

JAMES THURBER, in *Fables for Our Times,* retold the story of Little Red Riding Hood but modernized the ending. The dear girl, seeing the wolf disguised as Grandma in bed, whipped out her pistol and shot the impostor dead. After all, it takes more than a lace nightcap to make a wolf look like your grandmother, and the author points out that "It's not as easy to fool little girls as it used to be."

Thurber was also shooting down a time-worn literary device often called a "paper dragon." These tissue monsters are traditional and satisfactory in fairy tales; sometimes they work in adult fantasy or broadly humorous pieces. But in today's realistic, sophisticated fiction the presence of such a creature is usually fatal.

A paper dragon is a problem, situation, or solution that exists only on paper, never in life. To put it another way, it is something a writer dreams up or fetches from afar for the purpose of writing a story. One example may be worth a dozen definitions:

Richard Davis, a prosperous businessman, married an unattractive woman in the mistaken belief she was rich. Now he and his lovely receptionist are in love, so he plots to eliminate Mrs. Davis by murderously wielding a blunt instrument.

This plot, as it stands, will not pass muster. Has Mr. Davis never heard of divorce? Most people find this a better solution than homicide. Even if the wife opposes such action, prosperous Richard Davis can very likely find a legal way out of his marital misery. The problem, unless we provide a different motive, is not so extreme as the author would have us believe. Given present-day laws and mores, the tale, unless repaired, is a writer's hoax—a paper dragon.

Numerous paper dragon subspecies plague writers, but in my experience three distinct varieties are especially common and dangerous to effective fiction.

1. The false note

This is a single, improbable action that happens in the middle of an otherwise valid story. It may arise in any type of fiction, but suspense stories seem to invite this difficulty.

Recently I read a quite good but as yet unpublished romantic novel of suspense, a "gothic." At one point the heroine descends a dark stairway into the spooky cellars of a chateau. She knows very well that cellars are dangerous, but goes right on, impelled only by curiosity. Since this girl is aware that the dank rooms below are either haunted or dangerous and there is a chance that a fugitive criminal is hiding there, her conduct is idiotic. We realize at once that the writer is moving his character like a chess piece for purposes of plot. The heroine made this foolish descent only on paper, not in reality.

I suspect the writer was so carried away by the suspense he thought he was creating that he never bothered to give the girl a strong motive for rashness. There can be no suspense without believability, and the writer who frequently employs false notes to generate excitement is deceiving only himself, not his readers.

2. Obsolete dragons

Sometimes current events, changes in laws, and the discoveries of science will turn a valid fictional situation into just paper almost overnight.

In 1970, Irving Wallace published a commercially successful novel called *The Seven Minutes.* The story involved a trial resulting from the publication of an allegedly pornographic book, and the basic issue was freedom of expression versus the protection of public morality. Mr. Wallace's fans are probably so legion that nothing could have impeded the book's wide sale, but an unknown author attempting to use the same issue today would, in my opinion, be courting disaster.

The courts have settled the question of pornography in literature at least to the extent that the legal prosecution Mr. Wallace described would simply not happen today, except in a novel. No doubt it was a valid idea when the writer first thought of it; it had become less plausible by the time the book was published, and a year later had become an historical problem, not a contemporary one.

Some years ago I became fascinated with the notion of writing a novel about the moral ordeal of a college professor faced with having to sign a loyalty oath. Slowly the characters appeared in my mind, and slowly—too slowly —I evolved a background. By the time I was ready to start Chapter One, my perfectly good fictional problem had turned to foolscap. Academic loyalty oaths were ruled unconstitutional, and my projected book was suddenly transformed into a period piece—which was not at all what I wanted to write.

A long time elapses between a novel's conception and publication, and a writer, as I sadly learned, must either work very quickly or be sure he has chosen an issue that will not be rendered obsolete by tomorrow's headlines.

I do not mean that fiction must be about current or topical events—historical situations provide a treasure trove for authors. But yesterday's problems are ridiculous when tricked out in today's clothes. For instance, some novice authors still ignore the existence of The Pill when writing a story about unwanted pregnancy. Preventive measures would, of course, destroy some neat plot, so they overlook a discovery known to all the world, and never explain the character's ignorance, carelessness, or the accidental nature of what happened. Such pretense will not succeed. The facts must be explained and dealt with, not brushed aside.

3. Antique paper dragons

Years ago during the heyday of Hollywood romance, one paper plot was filmed in so many versions that the gist of it is familiar to everyone:

Miss Prim is a mousy secretary who loves her handsome boss, John D. Rochester III, a millionaire playboy. He, naturally, pays little attention to colorless Miss Prim until the day she takes off her horn-rimmed glasses and changes her hairdo. *Presto!* The ugly duckling was lovely Irene Dunne in disguise! The boss proposes marriage on the spot. "Darling . . . how could I have been so blind?" How, indeed!

This dragon, more fragile than onionskin, provided mass entertainment in its own day, although critics pointed out that ravishing beauty is not easily hidden under spectacles and braids in a bun, nor does a quick visit to Elizabeth Arden's revolutionize life.

Perceptive writers know that yesterday's mechanical stories are now hopeless. A few writers can still pass off shoddy, antique plots in the nether regions of TV situation comedy, but not in books or magazines. Authors may still use an improbable but fascinating coincidence, and readers will stretch their credulity for the sake of a rattling good story. Nevertheless, these same readers are the best educated, most sophisticated mass audience authors have ever faced. They have spent more time in school than their parents did, they are more widely traveled; television has taken them to the battlefields of Viet Nam and to the wastes of the moon. These people are not easily taken in by fictional tricks.

This is hardly an original observation. Most writers would agree that popular fiction, in general, is more mature than it used to be. But belief and practice are two different things, and each year I read more than a score of unpublished manuscripts by authors who still expect readers to believe that a wolf in a nightgown resembles Grandma.

Here is a recent example produced by a rather talented writer:

Mary Jones, a happy housewife, is sure that her husband John is faithful to her until the day she sniffs a strange perfume on his suit coat. Who is the other woman? Mary shadows John, checks up on him by telephone, and for a few days endures a hell of jealous insecurity. Then all is happily solved when John gives her a bottle of the mysterious perfume as an anniversary present. Surprise! He had carried it home in his pocket and hidden it until the big day!

One glance exposes this tale as pure paper. Mary Jones isn't supposed to be a neurotically jealous woman, but it takes only one faint whiff to send her into frenzy. And, above all, the whole story is just too pat to be true. If this is a happy marriage, didn't the thought of perfume as an anniversary gift cross the wife's mind? Of course it would in life. The whole thing is nonsense.

How can an intelligent writer be blind to such glaring falsity? It is only human to ignore weaknesses in one's own work, but I am convinced that is not the entire problem. *Writers who produce paper plots are drawing inspiration and ideas from fiction, not life.* This approach is bound to lead to implausibility, for the author is unconsciously saying, "This is the way things happen in stories. Real life is a different matter, and I needn't worry about it."

This view, never artistically valid, had some commercial justification in the bygone days when there really were "women's slick stories" and "formula adventure yarns." Writer-mechanics of a generation ago did not produce literature, but they made money when Miss Prim threw away her repulsive glasses.

Today, the older type of slick fiction with its paper dragons and ready-to-wear psychology has all but vanished. The ghost still walks, but only in a few television potboilers and in the work of a few older novelists who continue to sell, but in diminished volume, because their names are known to millions. Formula writing is a sterile field for a new writer.

The change in public taste has affected every area of fiction. *McCall's,* a magazine once known as the very epitome of "women's slick," has recently printed excerpts from three new novels, all of which enjoyed subsequent critical success as books. In examining six issues of that magazine, I found not one specimen of a "paper doll boy meets paper doll girl, and they are later hitched with a cute paper twist."

Much science fiction was once called "space opera" by its own writers because the plots were classic "horse opera," cowboy and cattle rustler yarns decked in the atomic trappings of the future. Some of these stories are still printed, but they are giving way to works richer in symbolism, philosophy, and genuine science. Confession stories, once the impregnable stronghold of formula writing, have moved toward greater sophistication, greater plausibility. In the detection field, no new Sherlock Holmes reconstructs a universe from some tobacco ashes.

Writers are constantly urged to read and study current trends. But this invaluable advice is useless if the writer reads while blinded by wishful thinking. When an author has written or intends to write a tricky, mechanical story, somewhere he will find evidence to raise false hopes for its success. One can always discover an exception, a paper dragon that has slithered into print. But the plain fact remains: implausible twists, puppet-like characters, and pat solutions are only antique paper, a drug on the market.

Slaying dragons

Paracelsus, the fifteenth-century physician who did much to establish modern medical science, made a youthful resolution which could not be more timely. He spoke of medicine, but I apply his words to writing. "How would I set about to learn this art?" he asked. "No other place but in the great open book of nature written by the finger of God!"

This surely sums up the matter. The author whose work is grounded in reality is always on the right road. He may lose his way, he may wander into blind alleys, but if he is truly drawing from life, he has at least the chance of producing something besides paper.

I do not mean he should be bound by pedestrian naturalism. Far from it! Successful fiction is dependent on the scope of the author's imagination. The writer's view of life may be whimsical, romantic, or dolefully pessimistic. But it must be his own view, not reality seen through someone else's spectacles.

When I examine my own manuscripts, trying hard to stare with a cold eye, struggling to ferret out paper dragons that have crept in, I believe I unconsciously think of a remark made in Jean Giraudoux's play *The Madwoman of Chaillot*. In the second act, a zany lady relates an improbable story. Another character brings her up short by saying, in effect, "Now tell us the truth! Did that really happen—or did you read it in a book somewhere?"

That question is so basic to a good fiction writer that he must ask it of himself over and over again. He must not be satisfied until he can reply confidently, "Yes, it happened. Not in my daily life, perhaps. But it is real because I sincerely felt these emotions. I truly lived the events in my imagination. I am honest."

Facing this question is not easy. It means turning away from one's favorite mechanical plot, and shunning superficial glibness and mere cleverness. But the modern reader has already rejected most far-fetched artificiality and has learned to recognize a paper dragon for the flameless creation it is. Surely a modern writer can do no less.

~ 10 ~

MENTAL TRANSPORTATION

GETTING in and out of the mind of a fictional character often causes problems in third-person writing. We shall consider only one aspect of the far larger subject commonly called "point of view" or "viewpoint." Point of view is such a major matter in fiction writing and so essential for an author to understand that an entire book could be devoted to it. For our purposes, we shall confine our attention to the troubles that sometimes beset a writer when he wishes to enter and later leave the mind of one of his characters, and we shall call the process "mental transportation."

In first person, the "I" narrative, no difficulties of this sort arise. The reader is always sharing the thoughts and impressions of "I." He is always inside "I's" head, hearing, seeing, and thinking. This is one of the strengths and simplicities of first-person fiction. It is also a limitation, since "I" cannot know exactly what "he" is thinking except by inference unless "I" is gifted with ESP or "he" tells his thoughts.

Third-person fiction is another matter. The writer becomes ringmaster of a four-ring circus: He is handling atmosphere, action, dialogue, *plus* the thoughts of at least one character and perhaps several. The writer wants to make a smooth entrance into the mind of a character, reveal his intimate thoughts, then achieve a subtle exit. A good author *glides* in and out—he does not leap, does not jar the reader.

The problems in controlling mental transportation in fiction writing have brought anguish to many beginning writers who do not realize that mastery of the techniques involved is required. They blunder ahead and often produce choppy writing with misplaced emphasis.

"How do I tell the reader what John is thinking?" a writer asks himself, gnawing his pencil. "Do I just say 'he thought' all the time? Do I shift to the first person when someone is thinking? Maybe I should put the thoughts in italics. Isn't it a good idea to change from the past to the present tense when reporting direct thoughts?"

All these questions, except in unusually complex works, are not so forbidding as an insecure writer often believes. There are good methods and bad methods of making mental entrances and exits. While everything always depends on the author's own taste and judgment, we still have some well-established principles that will serve as guidelines. The writer who understands these principles and adheres to them will find himself on solid ground.

The best and simplest way to acquire smoothness in reporting a character's thoughts is to give careful attention to the techniques employed by good fiction writers: analyze several stories and books.

Fiction written in the first person will not be helpful, since the methods are different and direct. Nor can we use those works generally called "stream of consciousness" as examples of how an author gets in and out of the minds of characters. This school of writing, which has had a tremendous impact on modern fiction, has become as old-fashioned as the Victorian novel. Newer works offer the writer better models, better material for analysis.

Guidelines

The ideas and suggestions that follow are not substitutes for analyzing the methods fine authors have used to solve the problems of mental transportation. They are, rather, a supplement and condensation of what the writer will find for himself when he examines effective fiction. Nor are they "rules" like the laws of mathematics. A "rule" in fiction, we repeat, is merely a description of how much excellent writing has been done, not how it *must* be done, not an inviolate law.

1. Avoid unnecessary shifts into the first person, especially when a character's thoughts are brief and undramatic. Here is an example of what *not* to do, a case of needless and awkward gear shifting:

> John looked at the girl with faint interest. I rather like her, he thought. I don't know quite why. He smiled and said, "Good morning."
> She returned his greeting. I suppose she's an art student, he mused. This neighborhood is full of them. I really haven't much in common with art students. He glanced down the street to see if his bus was coming.

The first paragraph of this example is not too bad, even though the change of person and the "he thought" are unnecessary. The second paragraph is much jerkier, and the juxtaposition of "he thought" and "he mused" shows awkwardness of style. Better rewrite the passage in the third person!

> John looked at the girl with faint interest. He rather liked her, but didn't know quite why. He smiled and said, "Good morning."
> She returned his greeting. John supposed she was an art student—this neighborhood was full of them—and he really hadn't much in common with art students. He glanced down the street to see if his bus was coming.

The rewrite is far smoother than the original. More important, it avoids the unwanted emphasis that "I" gives to a thought. A change into the first person underscores the idea that follows, giving it special prominence. John's reactions in this example are not strong. It is wiser to save the shift to the first person for a moment when real force is needed. For instance:

> John looked at the girl with loathing. I hate her, he thought. I'd like to strangle her! But he smiled and said, "Good morning."

Here we have sacrificed a little smoothness for the added stress that "I" and the exact words of a thought yield. If we change this paragraph as we did in the earlier example, some force will be lost.

But putting a thought into the first person gives added emphasis only if the technique is not used too often. If almost all thinking in a story is cast into the first-person mold, the result is not emphasis but awkwardness. It is like filling page after page with exclamation points. After a while the reader gets used to having the author cry, "Wolf!" and pays no attention.

Most stories, even the very modern and experimental,

are told in the past tense. You will notice in the foregoing examples that when thoughts are put into the first person, the tense changes to the present: "He rather liked her" becomes "I rather like her." This shift is another reason why thoughts expressed in first person stand out on a page. The stand-out quality, if overused or employed when no strong stress is intended, results in jerky writing.

The important point is not that either of the techniques shown above is superior to the other. But they are *different,* and have different purposes. The "straight" third-person method of expressing thoughts usually produces a smoother, more easily readable style. Shifting to "I" gives greater emphasis, but tends to be awkward if not done skillfully.

Let us consider two more examples. The first is with the "I" shift:

> Joe Conners leaned against the dock rail watching the newcomers dismount from the tour bus. He was a grizzled New Englander, gnarled as a shoreline tree. I can't stand tourists, he thought. I never did take to the summer people. I call them invaders!

Now here is a rewrite done "straight" in the third person:

> Joe Conners leaned against the dock rail watching the newcomers dismount from the tour bus. He was a grizzled New Englander, gnarled as a shoreline tree. Joe scowled at the tourists. He had never taken to the summer people and he called them invaders. Invaders!

To my mind, the overall effect of the rewrite is much better than the original. By using "scowled" instead of "I can't stand" it shows us something instead of merely telling it. And the rewrite is smoother. But, admittedly, we are not quite so much "inside Joe's head."

The moral for an author is: Each of the two methods produces a different effect.

2. Experiment with "fragmented sentences" to convey a character's thoughts.

People seldom think in neat, complete sentences. If you look out in the morning and see glorious sunshine, you are likely to say to yourself, "Beautiful," or, "A beautiful day." You will probably not think, "It is a beautiful day."

Fiction writers have long been aware of this, and one effective way to show a character's thoughts lies in the use of the "fragmented sentence." (Also called the elliptical sentence.)

Here is how it works:

> Miss Martin entered the hotel lobby and glanced around. No sign of comfort or hospitality. A worn leather couch, a bridge lamp with a battered shade, and a threadbare carpet. A depressing cave. But what else would you expect from an innkeeper like Matt Bowers? Had he ever thought of brightening it up? Not likely!

In this passage we are clearly in the mind of Miss Martin, and we are receiving impressions as they come to her. The lack of grammatical subjects and predicates in some of the sentences gives an effect of "thinking." So do the two self-asked questions.

If we rewrite the passage without any "fragmenting," the effect will be quite different:

> Miss Martin entered the hotel lobby and glanced around. There was no sign of comfort or hospitality. She saw a worn leather couch, a bridge lamp with a battered shade, and a

threadbare carpet. It was a depressing cave, typical of the character of its owner, Matt Bowers. He had never thought of brightening it up.

The rewrite is far more "external" than the original. Although we are seeing the lobby from Miss Martin's viewpoint, we are no longer in her mind. The effect is more formal, and a bit stilted.

In the first version, it was not necessary to write, "Miss Martin thought . . ." The fragmented sentences have done the job of tuning us in on her mind without the author's having to say anything about it.

This technique is so common in modern writing that it is easy to find excellent models for analysis. One of the best I know in the short story field is Conrad Aiken's "The Impulse." A superb demonstration of this method is found in the first chapter of Brian Moore's small modern masterpiece *The Lonely Passion of Judith Hearne.* Moore is not only a fine novelist, but no less than a wizard when it comes to gliding in and out of the minds of his characters:

> The street outside was a university bywater, once a good residential area, which had lately been reduced to the level of taking in paying guests. Miss Hearne stared at the houses opposite and thought of her aunt's day when there were only private families in this street, at least one maid to every house, and dinner was at night, not at noon. All gone now, all those people dead and all the houses partitioned off into flats, the bedrooms cut in two, kitchenettes jammed into linen closets, linoleum on the floors and "To Let" cards in the bay windows. Like this house, she thought. This bed-sittingroom must have been the master bedroom. Or even a drawingroom. And look at it now. She turned from the window to the photograph on the mantelpiece. All changed, she told it, all changed since your day. And I'm the one who has to put up with it.

Brian Moore writes so deftly that in the paragraph above we are not aware that he has employed four different techniques of revealing Miss Hearne's direct thoughts. He starts with the traditional "thought of" and "she thought." Then he launches into fragmented sentences, followed by the device of his character speaking to a photograph. When he makes the final shift into the first person "I," it is smooth and natural because we are used to being inside Miss Hearne's mind.

3. *Avoid interrupting a character's thoughts within a paragraph.* The following example will make the reason for this warning clear. First, here is what *not* to do:

> Marion sat on the steel folding chair at the edge of the dance floor. Why am I here, she thought. I don't belong in this place. The music of the rock combo assaulted her ears. Why did I let Mother nag me into coming? The lights from the flashing chandelier were blinding. I always give in to her, always, because she knows how to hurt me, make me feel ashamed.

This paragraph is as jumpy as a flea-circus. Marion's thoughts are brief, yet they are twice interrupted by descriptions of the scene. This involves constant shifts from third person to the first, then back again. A rewrite is called for:

> Marion sat on the steel folding chair at the edge of the dance floor. The music of the rock combo assaulted her ears and the lights flashing from the revolving chandelier were blinding.
> Why am I here, she thought. I don't belong in this place! Why did I let Mother nag me into coming? I always give in to her, always, because she knows how to hurt me, make me feel ashamed.

The rewrite is vastly better than the original. The sensation of being jerked in and out of Marion's mind has been eliminated, so the thoughts flow smoothly. An obvious moral: Set the scene, enter the mind, and stay there until the point has been made. Then—and only then—return to the "outer world."

Of course there are exceptions. One might want to build a sort of counterpoint of thought and outer events. But usually when we are jerked from mind to background and then thrust into thoughts again the cause is faulty technique, not artistic intention.

4. Be wary of using italics or other typographical devices to set thoughts apart, or for emphasis.

Many writers have experimented with the method of putting thoughts or memories in italics, and in the vast majority of cases the experiments fail.

An example of a successful attempt is William Faulkner's story "Barn Burning." But Faulkner's use of italic type for expressing thoughts is judicious and sparing:

> The store in which the Justice of the Peace's court was sitting smelled of cheese. The boy, crouched on his nail keg at the back of the crowded room, knew he smelled cheese, and more: from where he sat he could see the ranked shelves close-packed with the solid, squat, dynamic shapes of tin cans whose labels his stomach read, not from the lettering which meant nothing to his mind, but from the scarlet devils and the silver curve of fish—this, the cheese which he knew he smelled and the hermetic meat which his intestines believed he smelled coming in intermittent gusts momentary and brief between the other constant one, the smell and sense just a little of fear because mostly of despair and grief, the old fierce pull of blood. He could not see the table where the Justice sat and before which his father and his father's enemy (*our enemy* he thought in that despair; *ourn! mine and hisn both! He's my father!*) stood, but he could hear them. . . .

Beginning writers often underscore almost everything (this will be italicized in type), somehow expecting the printed form to give their stories force and effect. (These same people tend to overuse exclamation points.) This device will not work. The reader's eye becomes wearied by a jumble of type, and soon he becomes impatient with an author who is affected rather than effective.

5. Don't bend over backwards to avoid the words "he thought." The verb "thought" is much like the verb "said." A reader's gaze passes over it as if it were a punctuation mark. Saying "he thought" is usually the best and most natural way of announcing our entrance into a character's mind.

There are many good substitutes such as "he told himself" and "he decided." But in reporting a character's direct thoughts, a writer may become ridiculous if he dredges up unlikely synonyms. For instance:

> "There were many ways of doing it," he pondered.
> "It was a different matter," he puzzled.
> "Perhaps what she said was true," he considered.

These barbaric usages should be banned by law, and they are all catastrophes resulting from avoidance of the simple word "thought." Such verbs as pondered, puzzled, and considered are fine for indirect reporting of what goes on in a character's mind: "He pondered the many ways of doing it" or "He puzzled about this difficult matter." But those words are useless if we are telling the thoughts word for word.

In entering and leaving a character's mind the simplest, least obtrusive way is almost always the best. The principle behind this remark applies to practically everything in the writing of fiction.

~ 11 ~

DEVICES OF SUSPENSE

WE all read books and stories that we "just can't put down." On the other hand, many works, although meaningful and in some ways well-written, fail to keep us turning pages half the night. The difference is a matter of *suspense.*

Suspense permeates all good fiction (and the most readable nonfiction as well). It should spring from every element of a story—action, atmosphere and especially from characterization.

Generations of storytellers have worked out a number of literary devices to whet a reader's appetite for more and keep attention from flagging. The seven techniques for building suspense I will describe here are such devices.

They will not by themselves transform bad fiction into good, but they are definitely helpful, and this is proved by the fact that excellent writers of all generations have employed them to hold a reader's interest.

Some of these methods are commonly called "plants"

and others are known as "foreshadowing." Here are seven specific examples:

1. *The Mary Roberts Rinehart,* or, *"Had I But Known . . ."* Mrs. Rinehart, who was the queen of American mystery fiction for two decades, did not invent the technique of "had I but known," yet she used it so frequently (and sometimes so blatantly) that the device might well bear her name. Here is an example of the method:

> "I don't care what you say," said Julia, her eyes flashing. "I'm going to Bridge House to have this out with Arthur once and for all!"
> I watched her stride angrily down the path, the shortcut that led through the woods. She was detestable, I thought. Worthless. Yet despite my anger, I would have raced after her, begged her to stay with me, had I but known the fate that awaited Julia on the shadowy path to Bridge House.

The "Had I But Known" promises violence and terror to come. It was a useful suspense-builder two generations ago, and it is useful today. But the words "had I but known" are practically taboo in modern fiction! The technique in its original form has become cliché.

Does this mean the modern writer should avoid "had I but knowns"? Not at all. He simply must use the device in a more subtle form. Below is an example from Gore Vidal's short story "Erlinda and Mr. Coffin."

In this story a prim, prejudiced landlady complains to a new roomer, Mr. Coffin, that his eight-year-old ward, who has just arrived to live with him, is "a person of color." Mr. Coffin replies:

> ". . . if it offends your sensibilities, we will seek lodgings elsewhere."

Vidal then executes a neat variation of "Had I But Known" when the landlady wails to the reader:

Oh, what insane impulse made me reject this gesture of his? What flurry of *noblesse oblige* in my breast caused me suddenly to refuse even to entertain such a contingency! I do not know . . .

She may not know, but *we* know very well that the landlady is headed for trouble. She has in effect said, "Had I but known then what I know now, I would have acted differently."

British novelist Rumer Godden uses the same technique in a very different manner, suddenly skipping ahead in time to say, in effect, "Years afterwards she would be astonished that she could have been so foolish." (This is not a quotation but a paraphrase. Rumer Godden's method is too complex for brief summary.)

There are, of course, dozens of ways of using "Had I But Known" without writing those exact words: "I would not learn the truth until long afterward." [Had I but known.] "If Harry had not been so naïve, he would have behaved less recklessly that morning." [Had Harry but known!] "When Mary frowned at the old man, she had no reason to suspect that such a small unkindness would change her entire life." [Had Mary but known!] Such statements are intriguing and they urge the reader to continue because he has been promised that something is going to happen. Something of consequence.

2. Promissory words. In his book *Venture to the Interior*, Laurens Van Der Post writes, ". . . My grandmother was cradled, if not actually born, in an ox-wagon driving in the thirties of the last century into the unknown interior of Southern Africa. The ox-wagon was part of the small and ill-fated Liebenberg Trek . . ." The suspense here rests almost entirely on "ill-fated." Something terrible—and probably exciting—is going to happen to this wagon train, and we will assuredly read on to find out what. If you cut "ill-fated" the suspense plummets.

Compare these two sentences:

1. The sloop *Argus* began her voyage on May 5.
2. The sloop *Argus* began her unlucky voyage on May 5.

The adjective "unlucky" has promised us interesting events if we will continue reading. The single word makes the difference between an ordinary statement and an intriguing one.

The writer has available an endless supply of "promissory words." Some of the most effective seem to suggest misfortune. Certainly interest pricks up when we see such words as "a doomed expedition," "a fatal meeting," "a hazardous trip," or "a harrowing experience."

One should not think, however, that the use of promissory words is confined to adventure stories or works about violence. The "harrowing experience" may be entirely psychological, and a "doomed expedition" could be a trip into one's own mind.

3. Arousing readers' suspicions. If in a story you come across the sentence, "Beautiful Barbara Ames had everything to live for," you know instantly that beautiful Barbara is not long for this world, or at best she will soon face some danger or disaster. The writer has aroused our suspicions—and hopefully our interest. A reader knows very well that if Barbara is going to survive, his attention will not be directed toward her reasons for living.

Precisely the same sort of thing happens if we read, "Casual acquaintances considered Gerald Pope an honest man." We come to an instant conclusion: Gerald is a crook. Our attention has been directed toward honesty, and our suspicions aroused by the words "casual acquaintances." Obviously those who know Gerald better have detected his fraudulence.

This device of arousing a reader's suspicions was used by Somerset Maugham to open *Moon and Sixpence*. The author "confesses" that when he met Charles Strickland, he did not find the man extraordinary. Why the word "confess"? The writer is signaling the reader, and the signal says, "Strickland *was* quite extraordinary. Read on! You'll learn more about it."

Carson McCullers did this when she stressed the dullness and quietness of a military post during peacetime at the very beginning of *Reflections in a Golden Eye*. Will an author admit on page one that he is going to write about dull people in a dull situation? Of course not. So we know this military post will turn out to be anything but quiet.

Always our suspicions are aroused by a writer's apparent disclaimers. As an example: "It was a beautiful afternoon. A day so lovely, Jane thought, that no harshness or violence could intrude upon its peace." Well, Jane is mistaken. Trouble is just around the corner. If not, why would harshness and violence have been mentioned in the first place? The author is up to something and the reader knows it. Suspense is being built.

4. Suggestive objects. This is a sound and useful type of literary "plant." James Dickey in his novel *Deliverance* very early brings up the subject of archery: ". . . he could easily hold a sixty-pound bow at full draw for twenty seconds. I once saw him kill a quail with an aluminum target arrow at forty yards. . . ." Bows and arrows are mentioned not once but several times. And the reader, perhaps only unconsciously, realizes that someone or something is going to be shot with an arrow. Action and excitement are suggested.

If we are told that there is a loaded gun in a desk drawer, it may convey only character or atmosphere to us. But if the gun is mentioned a second or third time, however casually, it becomes a highly suggestive object. "Something will happen," we tell ourselves. "And it will involve that gun."

The object that excites our curiosity and consequently enhances suspense need not be anything so dangerous as an arrow or a gun. In Jean Stafford's excellent story, "A Country Love Story," the author "brings on" an old-fashioned sleigh. What, we wonder, is the meaning of this object upon which so much stress is placed? We read on to learn the answer.

In these two examples, the suggestive objects are essential to the works in which they appear. The plot of *Deliverance* requires archery, and in "A Country Love Story," the sleigh is a culminating and revealing symbol.

In a narrative where a shooting occurs, there must clearly be a gun. But if the gun appears only at the moment when it is needed for action, it has served no purpose in building suspense. A good opportunity may have been missed.

5. Prophetic symbols. These offer a good method of foreshadowing. In our culture, certain creatures and objects have definite meanings and are looked upon as omens. Vultures and skulls mean death; black cats suggest misfortune or witchcraft; a full moon often implies lust or mania, although it can mean love in certain situations. There are scores of such symbols, some obvious and others subtle.

The moment one of these symbols appears on the fictional horizon the reader knows that something is going to happen—they are plain forecasts ("foreshadowing") of action to come. If not used too cheaply and obviously, they are good attention-holders.

Earl Hamner, Jr. makes use of this technique beautifully and subtly in his novel *Fifty Roads to Town:*

> It had been night, and then it was day as the blood-red sun rose with a belligerent creaking in the eastern Virginia sky. The breeze which had worried the leaves of the dust-shrouded bushes along the highway exhausted itself, and the morning was quiet. The day was warm, even before the color of the sun changed from crimson to gold to yellow and then to a pale hot wine.

The writer has created a charged atmosphere. If one rewrites this passage cutting "blood" and "hot wine" and changing "dust-shrouded" to "dusty," the tension vanishes.

Joyce Carol Oates uses a prophetic symbol for the title of one of her stories, "Bloodstains." Before the reader has looked at the first sentence, the title has implied a promise of action. (In this case the "action" is almost entirely psychological—someone might even say "sociological"— but that does not matter. It is still action.)

Since readers are accustomed to prophetic symbols, one must be careful not to insert an object or natural event that can be mistaken for an omen when no such thing is intended. If a story or novel begins, "It rained on Joan Gordon's wedding day," a reader is inclined to take this as a storm signal of an unfortunate marriage. When no dark prediction is meant, the author had better improve the weather or point out that it was a soft, gentle rain awakening the sleeping earth.

6. *The impending event.* An impending event is some major thing that is going to take place in the future about

which the reader is informed in advance. It has many technical uses in fiction. For our present purposes we will consider only one facet—the impending event as it relates to the building of suspense.

Every reader who opens Bulwer-Lytton's classic, *The Last Days of Pompeii,* knows that a volcanic eruption of fearful might is impending. This gives the book built-in suspense. Who will escape and who will perish? Each page we turn brings us, we know, closer to the time when the mountain will explode.

However, impending events are not usually historical occurrences. My novel *The Flamingos* was constructed entirely around a series of impending events. At the beginning a group of characters board a bus. I hoped the reader would keep asking, "What will happen when these people arrive at their destination?" Upon their arrival, another impending event was immediately introduced, a concert to be held in the near future. Everyone talked about it, looked forward to it, made plans. I hoped the readers would be curious to learn what would happen when this much-heralded concert took place. But even before they went to the concert, I had planted the seeds of the final impending event, a disaster by wind and water.

I like to call this technique "Only Fifteen Shopping Days 'Til Christmas." As a child, I used to watch the front page of the local paper in December. There was always a little box that announced in bold type how many shopping days were left before Santa's arrival. My excitement mounted as the great event drew closer.

The same thing happens in fiction. Writers of pure suspense and thrillers have always employed this method. For instance: An innocent man has been convicted of a murder and is going to be hanged (the impending event).

A fictional detective must find the real killer before it is too late. He has only two weeks to accomplish this. Then only one week. Four days. Two days. And at the very last moment . . .

I once heard a hellfire-and-brimstone preacher use the same method at a huge revival meeting. His sermon told of the Biblical events on Calvary and the sufferings of Jesus. It started with dawn on the first Good Friday, and the preacher would intone, "six o'clock . . . seven o'clock . . . eight o'clock. . . ." It was a highly dramatic build-up to an impending event. In other words, "Only Fifteen Shopping Days 'Til Christmas."

7. *The mysterious refrain.* Of the many effective suspense techniques Carlos Fuentes uses in his novel, *The Death of Artemio Cruz,* one of my favorites might be called "the mysterious refrain." In this novel, a dying man speaks these words: "That morning I waited for him with happiness. We rode our horses across the river."

No one listening knows what the words mean, nor does the reader. Later they are repeated, but still without explanation. Then again. "Waited for whom?" we wonder. "What morning? What river? Why is this so important to a man on the brink of death?" Eventually we will learn the meaning; until we do our curiosity has been cleverly whetted.

In *The Inquisitor's House,* I used a less-often-repeated refrain, "Tante Julie, I love you." A man mumbled it in a recurring nightmare, then spoke it aloud. No explanation was given, and the reader did not learn who Tante Julie was for some time.

Muriel Spark built her novel *Memento Mori* around the refrain of a mysterious remark made several times over the telephone by an unknown caller.

Such a refrain need not be vocal. A character might suddenly find his thoughts turning to some unknown scene or object. He could remember or dream of such a thing as a broken toy soldier. Without his knowing why, the image could haunt him. In time he would arrive at an understanding or at least an explanation of this elusive memory. Meanwhile, the reader is also wondering about the toy. Curiosity has been aroused, suspense is built.

Writers of detective fiction especially love this device. A witness says something like, "There was something strange about the way the table was set. But I can't remember what was so peculiar. . . ." Later the witness's mind returns to the table. "Was it the wine bottle? No, something else." The witness never recovers his memory (until almost the end), but cannot erase the recollection of the table from his mind. Meanwhile, the detective-hero is doing much the same thing. A remark or an object has arrested his attention, but seems meaningless. Yet it worries him. His mind reverts to a cigarette burn in a carpet. What is he to make of it? It haunts him—it is a refrain. And it keeps the pages turning.

Handle with care

The seven techniques we have given for suspense-building must be used with caution and sincerity. If they are superimposed upon a story, tacked on, the results are artificial and melodramatic. One cannot save a bad piece of writing by dragging in flocks of vultures, an arsenal in a closet, or "Had I but known . . ." Nor is a boring work rescued by entitling it "The Lust-Mad Orgy."

Further, all these devices for generating suspense have one thing in common: they are *promises*. If a writer fails to keep such promises, his readers (who will be few!) have every reason to feel extreme annoyance.

When an author builds up the dangers of walking on Fourth Street at night and then sends his heroine down that thoroughfare in gloomy darkness, something must happen! Naturally, the action may be psychological, not physical. Or the point might be that everyone had exaggerated the peril. But the reader has been cheated if given a contrived build-up to nothing.

All forms of "plants" and foreshadowing are useful to a writer. But the "shadow" must be cast by something really impending; and even a literary "plant" must eventually bear solid fruit—otherwise it is useless and should be pruned from your story.

~ 12 ~

THE UNAVOIDABLE SITUATION

IN life when we are confronted with an unpleasant or potentially dangerous situation, most of us simply walk
away from it. We turn our backs, we withdraw. People
with good sense quickly leave a café where a brawl is
brewing, and do not wantonly antagonize persons who
can do them great damage. If one is strolling in the park
and overhears a husband and wife quarreling bitterly,
there is little reason to inject oneself gratuitously into
their wrangle. The scene presents what I call an "Avoidable Situation."

But even the most cautious soul cannot evade all life's
difficulties. We may enrage our employer because we are
compelled to demand a raise. A man's skull may be
cracked because his principles forced him to march in a
demonstration—or perhaps he was swept into the crowd
against his will. Such an occurrence is an "Unavoidable
Situation," and these situations are the *only* ones usable in
fiction if tension is to mount.

Maxim: When a character can easily withdraw from a

conflict or difficulty, no real suspense or tension is possible.

Not all modern short stories and novels are built around an Unavoidable Situation. Mood pieces, "slices of life," and literary experiments hard to classify sometimes find their way into print, usually in the "little magazines," less frequently in *The New Yorker,* rarely in other publications. A very few novels which have little conflict or character involvement are published each year. Some of them win critical praise, but the public usually votes "No" in the nation's bookshops. Today's readers seem to want character involvement and inevitability of plot (storyline), especially in longer works.

What, exactly, is an Unavoidable Situation that creates tension?

Let us say we are writing a story about a girl named Maggie, a waitress at a lunch counter. She hates her boss, she detests the customers, and she especially loathes the cook. Maggie's hatreds or her sufferings at the hands of others certainly offer possibilities for building tension and holding a reader's interest.

But what if Maggie can just quit the job any time she chooses? If she is a capable and attractive girl, she need not wait until the cook assaults her or the customers engender her nervous breakdown. Any reader will say to himself, "If she doesn't like it there, let her leave."

Now let us make Maggie's position *unavoidable.* She is *compelled* to continue because of her own nature: as much as she hates this job, it is familiar, and she is terrified of venturing into unknown surroundings. Further, for all her complaints, she actually enjoys subtly insulting the customers and making the cook's life hell. There are dozens of ways to force Maggie to remain, and a wise writer will make sure she is trapped.

To cite an example with which almost everyone is familiar, let us consider Mark Twain's *Huckleberry Finn*. At the very beginning, when Huck starts his memorable flight, he is compelled only to go far enough away to escape his brutal father. The moment the runaway slave, Jim, comes onto the scene all the circumstances change. Huck is now in an Unavoidable Situation which is fictionally perfect. Since it is not in Huck's nature to betray Jim, he is forced to continue his journey despite risks and difficulties. He cannot easily withdraw. Once this is established, suspense and tension become possible—and Mark Twain makes the most of it.

The tension of this particular storyline is heightened by the fact that Huck is tempted to act out of character. His instincts tell him to protect Jim, but he is not quite sure of himself. In a beautifully executed scene Huck is asked by slave hunters about the color of his unseen companion. It is a terrible moment for the boy—and a suspenseful one for the reader. Then Huck says, "He's white." The die is now cast; Huck is forced to see the situation through.

Great works of fiction, both old and new, are replete with the tension which springs from an Unavoidable Situation. In *The Grapes of Wrath* the Joad family cannot simply stop by the side of the road. Because of their circumstances and their faith, they must press on toward the promised land of California. Captain Ahab in *Moby Dick* cannot follow the sensible course of heading for port when the going gets rough; he is obsessed and driven. For a fictional character there is no turning back, no withdrawal, except at terrible cost to himself.

Many so-called "suspense novels" fail because their authors have done only half the job. They may create adequate characters, yet write a book without tension because they have placed their people in Avoidable Situations.

I have read three unpublished "police routine" novels that I am quite certain achieved no success because they *were* routine. It is hard to generate much excitement when a detective is investigating a crime merely because he is paid to do it. Some novice authors think it is enough to give their hero a job as a detective or policeman. This, they mistakenly feel, should automatically guarantee his emotional involvement in the crime they are going to write about.

But successful fictional detectives, from Sherlock Holmes to Roger West, have been fascinated, moved, and sometimes menaced in the course of their investigations. One of the best books of the Roger West series is John Creasey's *The Blind Spot* in which the detective and his family are directly under attack. Even money-hungry Nero Wolfe can be lifted from his armchair by an insult to his intelligence, a blow to his conceit or by an outrage to his principles—as in *The Doorbell Rang*. Georges Simenon goads his Inspector Maigret into deep involvement by many devices—pity for a potential victim, resentment of the Public Prosecutor, a critical observer from England.

All these fictional detectives, and other men of their profession in novels, find an unsolved crime a thorn in the flesh. They *must* go on, they *want* to go on. It is psychologically inconceivable that Nero Wolfe should shrug his fleshy shoulders and say, "I give up, Archie. This case is beyond the power of my intelligence." Rex Stout has created a character who, though slow in starting, rises to challenges and then, however much he sulks, finds himself in an Unavoidable Situation.

The principle of "no turning back" as an essential to

plotting is by no means confined to great novels and detective fiction. The highly popular romantic suspense
stories written by Mary Stewart, Victoria Holt, and others are firmly grounded in Unavoidable Situations. In
these books a sympathetic heroine usually takes a new
job or perhaps goes on a journey and trouble follows.
When she is threatened, why doesn't she simply quit the
job or go home? She cannot. Before she realizes the extent of her danger, she is already emotionally involved—
perhaps with a child or some other helpless person, perhaps romantically attracted to the hero.

Anyone planning such a novel should be very sure that
the heroine's emotional entrapment in the situation is
complete. Not long ago I read a rejected manuscript of a
"gothic," and it was easy to see why so many editors had
sent back the work.

The heroine, an attractive young secretary, had accepted a job in a gloomy old house on the New England
coast. Upon arrival there, she was insulted, abused and
threatened by a group of unpleasant characters. Any
woman with a grain of sense would have quit without notice. The situation was avoidable; the author failed.

The chain-link storyline

If life is "just one damned thing after another," then
well-written fiction is "just one damned thing *because* of
another." One of the challenges—and to me one of the
pleasures—of creating fiction lies in forging a storyline
which entraps the characters link by link. (It's best of all
when the characters seem to "do it themselves.") A small
event leads to a larger one, and gradually the Avoidable
becomes the Unavoidable.

William Gibson's novel, *The Cobweb*, begins when the
wife of the director of a mental institution orders new

draperies for one of the hospital's public rooms. It is a small, thoughtless act and completely avoidable, but the consequences become major. Characters are forced into positions and attitudes from which they can withdraw only at the price of humiliation or pain. Slowly but inevitably a chain reaction develops leading to a violent climax.

Today's best authors of realistic fiction, whether they are writing literature or confession stories, are masters at involving their characters, enmeshing them, trapping them in the Unavoidable.

All writers, novice or otherwise, can save wasted effort if they carefully examine a planned storyline from the standpoint of Unavoidability. If your characters, when pressure is put upon them, can calmly pick up their marbles and quit the game at no cost to themselves, then you are dealing with a situation which will be difficult if not impossible for effective fiction.

If Mr. Smith is cruelly persecuted by his employer, we must know why Smith does not leave this Simon Legree. The author who creates this situation must know and show why it is Unavoidable.

Acting out of character

The maxim we set down at the beginning of this chapter was: When a character can easily withdraw from a conflict or difficulty, no real suspense or tension is possible.

Before leaving the subject of the Unavoidable Situation, we must call attention to the key word in that sentence: "easily."

In life and in good fiction, people do surprising things. They act out of character, outwardly, at least. We have mentioned the tension Mark Twain created when Huck was on the verge of doing something contrary to his best instincts.

A fictional character *may* decide to pay the high price of escaping the seemingly Unavoidable, and this can come about either because of weakness or great strength. Fiction and drama, both old and new, are filled with characters who suddenly and astonishingly rebelled, or behaved in ways no one expected: *Herzog, Them, Moon and Sixpence, The Wall, The Adding Machine, The Glass Menagerie, The Fixer, The Wapshot Scandal.*

The situations of these characters were not, to themselves, as Unavoidable as they seemed to readers. Nevertheless, the people in the works mentioned were deeply and powerfully involved in the events of their stories.

A writer planning or rechecking any project in fiction must be certain that such involvement between the characters and situation exists in his own work. Can they easily turn away from difficulties? Does your detective detect merely because it's just another job or does he *care?* Can your "gothic" heroine easily give up her position as governess? Could the tormented, hen-pecked husband you've written about easily leave his shrewish wife?

If the answer to any such question is even a doubtful "Yes," then you will know you are handicapped by an Avoidable Situation. It is time to go back to the typewriter and make matters Unavoidable.

Length versus tension

When a writer reads what he hopes is a semi-final draft of a work he has produced and suspects that it is dull and lacking in tension, he usually starts cutting it. Words, sentences, paragraphs and pages are hacked from the manuscript.

Usually the author is right in doing this. Many themes,

ideas, and characters are simply not strong enough to bear a ton of wordage. Often tension and suspense are lost because the writer has strayed from the main point, or simply employed a lengthy and cumbersome way of saying something.

Today almost everyone likes compact writing. I myself happen to enjoy a more leisurely style in which there is ample time for charm and grace, but I realize my taste is not typical of most modern readers. Even some great classics, I admit ruefully, are more popular when abridged.

Nevertheless, young writers conditioned or even brainwashed by a Hemingway-like brevity can ruin their own work when they start slashing wildly with a blue pencil because something seems "boring." It is almost as if they were saying to themselves, "My ten-thousand-word story is dull. If I make it only five thousand words long, it will be only half as dull. At two thousand words only a fifth as dull, and by the time I've whittled it down to one thousand, I'll have a literary triumph."

This will not work. Certainly a story or novel may lack suspense and tension because it is too long for what it has to say. Unnecessary padding must be cut. On the other hand, too much cutting and condensing are every bit as dangerous as too little.

Since suspense derives far more from character and involvement than from mere outward action, a work may bore us because the character has never been established. In such cases, cutting will make the fiction worse, not better.

To be concrete, suppose you have just written a ten-page scene describing the final parting of John and Marcia, a couple who were once in love but have now decided they have no future together. John is packing his clothes and other possessions to move them from the apartment they shared while Marcia, the viewpoint character, watches or tries not to watch. It is a poignant situation and should have great tension.

When you read it over a second or third time, the scene strikes you as dull. Before you panic and reach for the blue pencil, consider carefully. Have you established Marcia as a woman? Have you shown the love she once felt and perhaps still feels? Do we know John? Do we understand how awkward this half hour is for him? If not, it will do little good to have him remove only eight objects instead of twelve. The trouble may be that the passage is too short, not too long.

Speed and brevity are not the automatic solutions to problems of suspense and tension. The character and his deep involvement with an Unavoidable Situation lie at the heart of the matter. When these are not fully established, cutting the length in half may not make the result less boring, but doubly so!

~ 13 ~

FICTION'S ALL-SEEING "I"

THE scene is a dull dinner party where conversation has lagged and the guests are glassy-eyed not from martinis but boredom. Suddenly someone says, "The strangest thing happened yesterday! I wouldn't have believed it if I hadn't seen it with my own eyes." Heads turn at once, everybody listens, and hope springs in the heart of the hostess. A storyteller has made a good beginning—so good that even if he is already a notorious bore he will hold attention for at least a few minutes. He has promised something extraordinary and that promise is powerfully backed by the words "with my own eyes." Nothing makes people prick up their ears as quickly as an eyewitness account. "I saw it, I heard it, and I can swear to it."

Many writers use the eyewitness or "I-witness" approach to a story because it offers initial advantages of credibility and immediacy. Moreover, the "I-witness" technique gives a sense of security to a writer who feels that not *too* much can go wrong if he employs a natural method of storytelling. And what is more natural than saying, "I looked out the window this morning and I saw . . ."

But this apparently safe method conceals its own special pitfalls for the unwary writer. I speak from sad experience. At least twice during my first year of producing short stories, I wrecked otherwise good tales on the rocks of the "I-witness" approach. If a shrewd critic had not pinpointed my basic mistake, I might not know to this day why those stories foundered. Since then I have had the rather grim consolation of learning that I was not alone in my sins. Reading the unpublished manuscripts of other writers, I have noted a repeated difficulty in handling the "I-witness" account. The danger, unique to this form of writing, lies in the treatment of the "I" character himself, a character who is all too often an unfleshed skeleton, starved because the author thought "I" could take care of himself and neglected him for the sake of "more important" characters. "I" is forgotten because, like the purloined letter and the famous "invisible postman," he is so obvious that the writer does not notice him.

To put the problem in the form of a question: In fiction, how do you handle an "I-witness" who tells the story when this witness is not the hero?

The role of I-witnesses

In first-person writing where "I" is not only the supposed author but also the central figure, there is no question about where to fit "I" in. He is always in the midst of everything; the story *belongs* to him, is about him. All confession magazine stories are pure "I" tales, not eyewitness accounts. So are the "I, Personally" nonfiction pieces in *Reader's Digest*; so are such classics as *Huckleberry Finn* and *Jane Eyre*, and such modern novels as *The Catcher in the Rye*.

In all of these "I the author-hero" stories, the narrator

dominates the action and thought. Here, the place of "I" is clear enough, and there is small danger of his suffering an author's neglect.

There are only a few precautions a writer should take, a few questions he should ask himself before he selects a particular character as "I the author-hero." These questions seem terribly obvious, and indeed they are—to everyone except an author who falls into a trap.

Is the "I-hero" sensitive and discerning enough to tell his own story? To return to a classic example, Huck Finn is shrewd about human nature and, although still a boy, highly aware of the world around him. By contrast, his friend Tom Sawyer is completely wrapped up in himself. Tom is too romantic, shallow, and boyish to see the world very clearly. Mark Twain wisely wrote *The Adventures of Tom Sawyer* in the third person but put *Huckleberry Finn* in the first. Tom was incapable of telling his own story while Huck was a superb narrator.

Is the "I-hero" an articulate type? The taciturn heroes which film actor John Wayne played on the screen for a generation are impossible storytellers. Their whole effect comes from the mysterious silence of "a man of deeds, not words." It is better to have someone else tell about this hero. (Can you imagine a book called *The Autobiography of Calvin Coolidge*? I suppose it would be half a page long.)

But, given a hero capable of telling the story, one has little doubt about where to put him: in the center of the stage with a large spotlight beamed upon him.

It is in the less straightforward narrative, where "I" is a witness but not the central figure, that the problem of giving him his proper place arises.

To be absolutely clear about what I mean by "I-witness" fiction, let me change an old nursery rhyme into prose. If it is to be a pure "I the author-hero" story, it comes out like this: "Call me Jack. Yesterday I went up the hill with my sister, Jill, to fetch water. I stumbled and suffered a skull fracture. My sister had a similar accident."

Now we change it to the "I-witness" form: "Yesterday while I was chopping wood in the yard, I saw Jack and Jill walk by carrying a pail. They climbed the hill, going up the path toward the well. Suddenly Jack tripped and rolled down, then the same thing happened to his sister." That is an "I-witness" speaking.

"I-witnesses" are commonly used by fiction writers in two very distinct ways: 1. "I" as a Notary Public; 2. "I" as an Accomplice and Reporter.

Before analyzing these uses, let us glance briefly at a very rare use of "I" in the novel. We might call it "I the author" and most English-speaking readers will know the method from only one book, *The French Lieutenant's Woman* by John Fowles. This book enjoyed such a huge sale a few years ago that I cannot imagine there exists a reader who has not at least heard of it and of the surprise device of the author's (or a character who said he was the author) suddenly injecting himself into the story to announce that this was, after all, just a novel and not real life. He, the author, could do what he liked with the tale, and at the end had not yet made up his mind about what "really" happened.

Since we are concerned with problems of writing and not the history of literature, I will say only that this device, which author Fowles used in his own special way, was certainly not as new as many startled readers thought it to be. The whole idea of proclaiming that "none of this is real" is both implicit and explicit in the plays of German dramatist Bertolt Brecht. Jean Genêt used another version of it with tremendous power and effect in *Our Lady of the Flowers*, a novel which soars to heights of beauty and plunges to depths of sheer disgust.

We have mentioned this unusual device for only one reason: it now, in the public's mind, belongs to John Fowles. Anyone who wants to use "I the author" as a technique must work out a very different approach from the one used in *The French Lieutenant's Woman*. The bloom is now off that particular rose, and some years must pass before it can reappear with apparent freshness.

Now let us return to the mainstream of "I" fiction.

"I" as a notary

The "I-notary" use is often more of a decoration or means of introduction than anything else. A notary in real life verifies documents, swears to authenticity, but usually plays no other role in the transaction he attests. His job is to provide proof.

In fiction, the "I-notary" device sometimes gives credence to an otherwise doubtful tale. The presence of "I" explains the origin of the story, tells how it came to light. He is the master of ceremonies who briefly introduces the main act and tries to give it a proper build-up.

To return to our nursery rhyme, an "I-notary" beginning might go like this: "Yesterday while searching the stacks of an ancient library I discovered a peculiar manuscript, parchment covered with curious writing in ink which was the brownish color of dried blood. It appeared to tell the story of a childhood tragedy, but the language was a rare dialect of Middle English, so I was not certain. Now, having spent the night translating, I will set down the tale exactly as it was related in that antique folio: 'Jack and Jill went up the hill to fetch a pail of water . . .' "

This is an "I-notary" at work, striving to catch our attention, struggling to give importance to a story.

An excellent example of this use of "I" is Gerald Kersh's blood-chilling story, "Men without Bones," which first appeared in *Esquire* and was later reprinted in the Alfred Hitchcock anthology, *Stories That Scared Even Me.*

Kersh begins his tale with the sentence: "We were loading bananas into the *Claire Dodge* when a feverish little fellow came aboard." By using "we" the writer has instantly provided at least one eyewitness, someone to swear to the fantastic story which follows. The author then briefly but effectively establishes his "I-notary" as an American aboard the ship who is startled by the strange appearance of the newcomer.

Fiction is not truth, and there is no more reason to believe the character "I" than to go along with an author who wrote, "Bananas were being loaded on the *Claire Dodge.*" But the effect of Kersh's using "we" is undeniable. It helps the writer achieve Coleridge's famed "suspension of disbelief." Kersh's "I-notary" gives an extra tone of truth to the tale.

After a short beginning passage, "Men without Bones" shifts into a first-person, "I the hero" story about astonishing adventures in Yucatan which are related by the feverish little fellow as he speaks to an *absolutely silent and unquestioning* listener. Only at the very end does the writer return to the deck of the *Claire Dodge* and bring back his "I-notary" character to wind things up and be the sounding board for a final effect. Through the entire mid-section, the bulk of the narrative, Kersh forgets his notary and so does the reader. If Kersh had allowed the "I-notary" to sneak onto the stage several times and divide the attention, the story would have suffered. Kersh did not permit this; he knew his craft.

The "I-notary" never tells the whole story in his own words. As a narrator he only repeats what someone else told him or presents a manuscript which he somehow discovered. In a short story it is usually not difficult to bring him on at the beginning and then get rid of him forever, or at least until near the end. In a novel this is more difficult, and even a great writer can have problems using the "I-notary" technique. As much as I admire Emily Brontë's *Wuthering Heights,* late in the book I find myself impatient to be finished with the author's "I-notary" and listener, a man who is the new tenant of Thrushcross Grange. I want to get on with the story of Cathy and Heathcliff and the young lovers, a story the housekeeper is telling as a perfect "I-witness." Miss Brontë's "I-notary" is blocking my view. Luckily, the author keeps these intrusions to a minimum. This quibble with a great novel serves as a warning to me never to let an "I" character who is only a notary and listener bob in and out of the action too much. The "I-notary" should leave quickly and quietly without causing confusion.

An "I-notary" story which anyone can easily obtain for examination is Edgar Allan Poe's classic "A Descent into the Maelstrom." An unidentified notary, assumed to be the author himself, accompanies an old man to the top of a cliff. A scene is set. Then the old man begins speaking *without interruption.* The notary character never again appears except by indirection at the very end of the story when the old man refers once to "you."

This is not natural, of course. In life, if someone is telling you a long story, you frequently break in with questions or exclamations. "Really?" "Amazing!" "What happened then?" Natural or not, this is to be avoided in "I-notary" fiction. Every time the notary injects himself into the action the mood is shattered, the spell the real narrator has been weaving is broken.

I suspect that writers who permit this to happen do it because they feel insecure. They are saying to themselves, perhaps unconsciously, "A person doesn't go on talking that long in life. The listener is sure to speak." But in this case life is no excuse. We are dealing with a literary convention, a method of storytelling that works very well. One tampers with it and makes it "natural" at his own risk.

The "I-notary" who discovers or receives a manuscript or maybe a collection of old letters, documents, and the like, is similar to the notary who merely listens. Use him and get rid of him.

A word of caution here: an original method of discovering the manuscript is needed. It must be imaginative but probable. So many "strange manuscripts" have been stuffed into bottles and later washed ashore that it's no wonder our beaches are covered with litter. And how familiar these words sound: "I had never until yesterday opened Grandfather Jordan's trunk that had gathered dust in the attic all these years . . ." Yes, a manuscript is about to be found, and in the same tired way.

The "found manuscript" is a rather trite device, and the writer who wants to use it for modern fiction must think of a clever idea. Two good examples from a few years ago are found in Robert Crichton's *The Secret of Santa Vittoria* and John Hersey's novel, *The Wall.*

Sometimes a story which does not quite make the grade otherwise can be improved by adding an "I-notary." It is worth looking again at a rejected manuscript to see if this is the case. One of my earliest efforts in short fiction was an imitation folktale clearly unsuitable for mass-circulation magazines. I submitted it to several rather modest publications, but it failed there, too. As a last resort I rewrote the beginning and a few sentences at the end, adding an "I-notary."

The original opening was: "In a village with the odd name Tlaquepaque there once lived a woman who was a notorious gossip and scandalmonger."

The rewritten lead became: "I first heard this unlikely story from my grandmother, a woman who always told the absolute truth despite a mischievous twinkle in her eye." There followed another paragraph describing how the story was told. In terms of overall length, the change was not great.

The story was accepted on its next submission. The personal touch at the beginning and again briefly at the end did the trick. It warmed the story up. If the tale had not been reasonably good in the first place, certainly the "I-notary" could not have saved it. But here was a case of an "almost" that needed a little touch to spell the difference between acceptance and rejection.

The accomplice-reporter

The second type of "I-witness" stories is the "I as an accomplice-reporter" group. This is fiction in which the "I" character, although he is not the hero, tells the entire story in "his own words," remains present throughout the work, and is the "all-seeing I." The author pretends to be "I" from beginning to end.

"I" may have a small physical role in terms of action, but he is in every scene, of course, even if only hiding behind the potted palms and presumably taking notes while he eavesdrops. Such older novels as Somerset

Maugham's *Moon and Sixpence* and *Cakes and Ale* use this technique of "I-witness," a man not the central character. Countless stories and novels are written as though reported by a housekeeper or an old family friend: *The Way of All Flesh, The Last Puritan,* and a thousand more of both today and yesterday.

A prime example of "I" as accomplice and reporter is Dr. Watson in the Sherlock Holmes stories. He is not only presented as the actual "writer" of every word, but he is also *involved*, hot on the trail with Sherlock, lagging behind but panting to keep up. He is in the action: he is tied to a chair, his life is often endangered, he searches for mysterious clues. As readers, we see and hear through Watson's eyes and ears, but the story remains Sherlock's. Watson is such an ideal "I-witness" character that one can find a dozen imitations of him in any bookstore.

Of the many points that could be made about writing this type of fiction, I wish to stress only one: If the "I-witness" is not just a notary but the teller of the whole story and present at every scene, then he must be involved up to his ears, emotionally as well as physically. "I" is a fictional character and must function like all other characters in the story. If his interest is only vague curiosity, then his presence will clutter the plot and divide the interest.

I do not mean that the "I" character must hog the scene. He need not do heroic deeds. But if he is there forever watching, as he must be if he is later to write the story, then "I" has to react as an alive and alert human being. "I" cannot be a mere tape recorder or a self-operating stenotype machine. If he is that, then the third-person approach will probably serve the story better and the colorless nonentity called "I" can be deleted.

This seems glaringly obvious, but my own experience

and my examination of other writers' work point to the
fact that the "I-witness" is all too often the last concern of
his creator. The author takes "I" for granted, and this
will not do at all.

Here let me report one of my greatest non-successes.
Several years ago I wrote a story called "Blessing of the
Animals." It told of primitive and often violent life in a
small Mexican village, and all action was seen through
the eyes of a young American who was the "I," the teller
of this first-person narrative. I had pictured this young
man as a self-effacing type, reserved, rather shy, a man
who seemed born to be a perpetual spectator. The story
was episodic: a scene in a native market, another in a
red-light district, another at a frenzied religious festival.

The young American, "I," was in no sense a hero or
central figure. This story was not about him; it was about
the life around him, the life he observed and reported.

I thought the tale was packed with colorful personalities and bizarre events. In previous months I had sold
half a dozen stories, two of them to magazines which
were quite snobbish editorially, and none of those stories,
I was sure, equaled this one. I cannot tell you how delighted I was with this work! It was a classic case of pride
going before a fall.

"Blessing of the Animals" was a finalist in a highly-
paid contest, but for some mysterious reason, it did not
win. It drew flattering notes from editors at *The New
Yorker, Esquire* and several other magazines. They did not
buy it. The story was never published and now it never
will be because much of it, in different form, went into
my first novel, *The Flamingos.*

When I later acquired a literary agent, I sent her the
manuscript, still not understanding the cause of its failure. She detected the weakness at once.

"Your 'I' character who tells the story is never really *moved* by anything. Nothing happens inside him. What he sees is interesting and comic and at times pathetic, but the reader remains on the outside because the narrator is on the outside. 'I' is only a spectator."

Only a spectator. That was precisely the trouble. My "I" was not a human guide for the reader, he was only a lifeless foreign object standing in the way. I had not wanted my "I-witness" to detract from the color around him, so I had made him so self-effacing that I had denied him life. He walked through the pages like a zombie.

I examined another story which had also failed, another "I-witness," and here I found the same lack. This "I-witness" was merely a stage manager with no role to play. Yet he was standing in the center of the stage while the necessary actors performed around him. He blocked everybody's view; he was an embarrassment to the audience.

Observe, record, reflect

Christopher Isherwood described himself as a writer in the famous line "I am a camera." This was not meant to be advice on the technique of writing. Isherwood's first-person writings are anything but impersonally photographic. "The camera" is forever taking part, reacting and understanding, involved with Sally Bowles and the landlady and his students—whirled into the life around him.

Yet I have heard the "I am a camera" text quoted by some beginning writers as the credo and theory of their work. This is a distortion of Isherwood's meaning. The sense of the passage from which the famous line comes is that the young writer must be constantly observant and later reflective.

Still, I quite agree that the "camera" notion describes what certain writers attempt to achieve. So cold an approach would not work for me in any form of fiction, yet admittedly it can sometimes have success in third-person narratives. But never in "I-witness" fiction.

In third-person writing, the "author is God," he knows all, sees all, and can peer into the minds and hearts of men with utter detachment—if he is that sort of God. The author acting as "God" can perhaps afford to be impersonal and unreacting at times. In an "I-witness" story such detachment by the "I" character is fatal. If "I" is only a camera with a tape recorder appended, then the story belongs in the third-person. "I" must be human and therefore concerned.

The "I-witness" need not be much involved at the beginning of a story. Often he is a bystander who is later drawn in. Graham Greene does this subtly and skillfully in *May We Borrow Your Husband?* Greene's "all-seeing I," a middle-aged Englishman, is at first only an accidental spectator with normal curiosity about an odd couple he observes in a hotel where he is staying. Gradually, because of the young wife's charms, the "I-witness" becomes drawn into the events he reports. It is this involvement that makes the story a success. If Greene had permitted the narrator to remain outside the action and unaffected, then his "I" would have been nothing but a Paul Pry repeating unsavory gossip. Involvement is the key.

Anyone who carefully analyzes successful "I-witness" fiction will be struck by the great number of emotions which the "I" storyteller, even if a minor character, feels. We have mentioned *Wuthering Heights.* Mrs. Dean, the housekeeper who tells most of the tale, is at different times worried, hopeful, anguished, frightened, rueful and happy. She is not nearly so colorful a personality as the violent hero and heroine she tells about, but she is always human, always living flesh and blood. The housekeeper has her own thoughts and feelings; she is not just a mirror for others to be reflected in, and never a "camera." The same things are true of Sherlock's Dr. Watson. And undoubtedly they will be true of the next good "I-witness" story or novel that is written.

Check List

For myself, when I work with the "I-witness" device, there are certain points I check carefully. I cannot pretend that I do this in so organized a fashion as I will set down here, for much self-criticism has to be an impression, an instinctive reaction, a gloomy suspicion about one's own weaknesses. But in a general way I look for answers to these questions:

1. If my "I" character is only a notary, do I really need him? Is he clutter? Should the story simply begin cold?

2. The reverse of that question. Could the story be strengthened by the introduction of someone who "saw it happen" or "had it told to him"? Do I want a verifier? An "I-notary"? (This matter needs special attention if the story is in any way fantastic. You will not find too many "I-notaries" in anthologies of "literary" stories; but they crop up all the time in collections of "hair-raisers.")

3. If my "I-witness" is an accomplice, the reporter who supposedly writes the story, then is he emotionally involved? Does he have a *real* reason for his concern about the events? (Idle curiosity will not do!)

4. Is my "I-witness" a living person with specific reactions? If he is a camera, perhaps the story belongs in the third-person form.

5. Is my "I-witness" a neglected orphan? Have I been so interested in the colorful people he watches that I've left him to waste away from malnutrition?

If my feelings about these matters are not reassuring, then it is time to return to the typewriter, "I-witness" story in hand. Once more the drudgery of rewriting, once more the exasperation of not getting it right the first, second, or tenth time. And, as always, the least improvement is well worth the effort.

~ 14 ~

MAGNIFICENT TRIFLES

IF I had a framed motto hanging over the desk where I struggle to create fiction, it would be a brief quotation from Michelangelo: *"Trifles make perfection, but perfection is no trifle."* The great sculptor-painter who toiled on his back for years to produce, brushstroke by brushstroke, the miracle that is the Sistine Chapel, knew this firsthand. To me, as a writer, his words have special meaning and value. I think they ought to be ingrained on the consciousness of anyone who hopes to write really well.

In the Michelangelo motto, as applied to writing, I find a double-barreled warning which an author ignores at his peril. First, there is *nothing,* however small, that a writer dares "pass over lightly" in his own work. Excellent writing is a matter of thousands of decisions, most of them minor. What word to use for exact meaning? What details to include? What to leave out? Not one of these choices can be made thoughtlessly or allowed to stand afterwards from sheer neglect or because "that detail isn't very important."

Second, little details, seemingly useless touches that I like to call "magnificent trifles," can sometimes glorify your writing—or ruin it. Your new story may have an ingenious plot; you may have invented a raft of lovable characters; but—speaking after my own struggles—if you have neglected the "trifles," the odds against your success are overwhelming. On the other hand, many a banal yarn has found its way into print simply because its author understood the handling of "trifles" and made them work for him.

What do I mean by "trifles"? I refer to little details that set a scene, reveal a character, lend reality to a situation, or make a subtle comment. In any writing, but especially in the short story, we do not have limitless space. Even if we had, most of us couldn't possibly fill it up with worthwhile material. Besides, a reader's time is limited, too. Since we must confine our wordage sharply, it is vital that every last detail be put to work and if possible to double labor. A short story cannot haul excess baggage— and a novel shouldn't.

Dramatic purpose

In speaking of the use and misuse of details, I will have to talk in terms of my own writing—not because it is so rich and textured, but because it is the only writing that I know fully inside and out. Before going into my own specific reasons for selecting or rejecting certain details, let me give an example of an absolutely first-rate use of a "trifle" by an author who can certainly be called "established." The Roman historian Suetonius, after two thousand years, still commands a large audience. More important, he has been read for sheer pleasure by generation after generation, not because he is profound or scholarly—he is neither. But he knew how to choose the right detail and then squeeze every drop of juice from it.

In *Lives of the Twelve Caesars,* he describes an assassination which changed the course of history. Julius Caesar, emperor of the world, has been felled by twenty-three stab wounds. Never in the memory of men has there been a murder of such tremendous consequence. Rome will plunge into civil war, the story of humanity will be altered. This is a scene of monumental importance— hardly the time for an author to indulge in details. But how does Suetonius end it? He writes: "All the conspirators made off, and he lay there lifeless for some time, until finally three common slaves put him on a litter and carried him home, with one arm hanging down."

With one arm hanging down. This, to me, is a magnificent trifle. The position of Caesar's arm, of course, is completely unimportant to history. But what a difference those five words make to the writing! We feel that Suetonius actually stood in the Roman Forum that day and watched the whole thing happen. He must have to have observed so small a detail. In reality, Caesar's murder took place a century before Suetonius was born, but by one touch of writing Suetonius has become an eyewitness, and we, as readers, are transported to the scene of the crime. If you cut those five historically inessential words, the passage loses its life, its magic, and becomes as dead as Caesar himself.

This "trifle" does its first job beautifully. It convinces the reader of the truth of the story—it makes him *believe.* But, doing double work, it also serves a dramatic purpose. In a few seconds the all-powerful Caesar has toppled from the throne of the world to the bloody stones of the Forum. His utter helplessness in death is ironic and pathetic. Suetonius could have written a thousand-word essay to show "how the mighty have fallen" and not made his point with the punch and clarity he achieves in one quick phrase when he shows the hand that once held human destiny dangling from a litter borne by slaves. Thus the writer, by one exact detail, has made five words do the work of a thousand, and his "trifle" has accomplished a second important job: it has made a subtle comment on the story.

The careful writer's use of detail to make his story vivid and convincing has not changed in the two thousand years since Suetonius. Examine any piece of good writing published today—whether in a literary review or a confession magazine—and you will find that much of its effect comes from apparently insignificant touches. You could cut most of them and not change the plot a bit. But if the author has done his job well, try cutting them and see what happens! The entire story will be lost.

I do not suggest that good writing results from the mere heaping on of details, however colorful they are in themselves. Quite the opposite! The writer who slathers trifles over his plot and people will soon find himself bogged in a mire of his own making. We have all read this sort of guff—waded through stories that made us long to poke the author with a cattle prod to force him to get on with the action. Too many "good" details are as bad as too few, and the author is always in danger of being a spendthrift or a miser. If he goes too far in either direction he will surely wind up being a bore.

To enrich or to clutter?

How, in a practical way, does a writer know when trifles are enriching his story and when they are simply cluttering it? Of course, the whole thing finally comes down to talent, judgment and critical taste. But for me there are certain working methods that seem to help and certain questions I repeatedly ask myself to guard against the misuse of details.

As a concrete example, let me describe the process of my writing a story called "Eskimo Pies" which first appeared in *The Atlantic Monthly* (January, 1964) and was reprinted in Martha Foley's *Best American Short Stories of 1965* and in other collections and textbooks. It is a story that owes whatever success it has had to details and trifles.

At the time I wrote "Eskimo Pies" I was not a beginning writer, but was certainly a novice in the field of fiction. Articles in *The Writer* magazine had advised me that *The Atlantic Monthly,* a publication I greatly admired, was sympathetic to new writers of fiction, so I spent three days analyzing every copy of *The Atlantic* I could get my hands on. It was painstaking, confusing work, for *Atlantic* fiction is diverse in content and style. But I discovered a common factor in most of the stories I read: they rang with truth. The authors achieved an impression of utter honesty, a "you are there" feeling, and they built real worlds around their characters by using graphic, sharp, true-to-life details. With this lesson in mind, I sat down to grapple with the first of many drafts of "Eskimo Pies," a basically simple story about a child's first exposure to the hard facts of the working world. It was not, as some readers have supposed, autobiographical.

Although I had studied fiction in *The Atlantic* and intended to send the story there first, I did not "slant it for a market." I made no attempt to write "an *Atlantic* story." I doubt that there is such a thing. I wanted to write a *good* story.

I worked then as I work now: I wrote a "bare bones" version. Earlier, I described writers who are too sparing of details as "misers." In my first drafts, I am an Ebenezer Scrooge. I record only the plain facts, the absolute essentials. Perhaps this is because of my background of newspaper writing, for my impression is that many writers work in the opposite way—they write long first drafts, then cut, edit, and revise. I could not do this. I must have a skeleton first, then try to give it flesh and—hopefully—life.

For me this is much the best working method. If I tell a story in the briefest way possible, I can see at once what the important issues are. (And if I really *have* any important issues!) Long, complicated first drafts can be confusing, a matter of not being able to see the forest for the trees. I do not claim that this is the only way to write; but I think it is a good way, an approach that reveals the essentials quickly.

After that first undecorated, undetailed version of "Eskimo Pies" was completed, I began the brainracking job of choosing and inserting the "trifles" that would make or break the story. The opening sentence reads: "During the worst of the depression we lived in a mustard-colored house on Majestic Boulevard in Columbus, Ohio." The first sentence brought two problems in the selection of detail. First, the color of the house. In writing and rewriting that sentence, I repainted that house a dozen times. It was brown, it was green, it was everything but purple striped. Finally, it was mustard-colored because that hue had the dinginess I wanted, and moreover, mustard has not only a color but a definite taste—acrid, bitter, faintly sour. I wanted to suggest all those things about the house without going into a long description. So I used a word that might, by implication, do more than one job.

Problem two was naming the street—"Majestic Boulevard." Perhaps to a casual reader the street's name was unimportant, but to me it was vital. "Eskimo Pies" tries to show the brutal difference between the real world and the world of poetry, romance, and imagination. Calling this slum street "Majestic Boulevard" seemed to add a bit, a trifle, to this theme. I made a similar choice later in the story. The climax occurs in a laundry, a dirty, ugly place, a chamber of horrors to a small boy. I called it the "Snow-White Laundry" because that name was everything the place was not and because "Snow-White" suggests a fairy tale, again carrying the story's theme forward in a small way. I also had the "Arden Ice-Cream Company" and "Camelot Road" to add a little more false romance.

Every sentence, every paragraph, involved similar choices and a constant search for details that would not only establish the setting and atmosphere as briefly as possible, but would also contribute to the overall meaning.

For instance, there is a scene in which the boy-hero and his mother read poetry aloud to each other. I cudgeled my memory and listed dozens of sounds, sights, and smells of a summer night in the Middle West. I wrote a long paragraph, much more than half a page. Then I found that most of these details were merely repetitious— they all said the same thing. I threw out practically all of them and ended up with this:

> The moth millers banged against the screens. The ancient electric fan buzzed fiercely and my grandfather's voice rang from the front of the house. "God gave the earth to man. Just how much of it do *you* own?" But my mother and I heard only my thin voice chanting, "This is the ship of pearl, which, poets feign,/Sails the unshadowed main . . ."

Why those particular details and not others? I chose "moth millers" because they suggest summertime and the name is middle western. When moths hurl themselves against screens they often kill themselves trying to reach the light inside. This advanced the story's meaning—the conflict between reality and poetic idealism. I hope no reader consciously thought of this—I detest the obvious use of "big, fat symbols." But the moth millers set my scene and—subtly, I hope—did a little more. The fan had to "buzz fiercely" because I needed an angry sound to contrast with the poem the boy was reading.

During one of the rewrites—I cannot remember which one—I realized that when I saw the action of the story in my mind it was rather like a black and white movie—no color. I rechecked the manuscript and found that this was true, that I had been very sparing in the use of adjectives describing colors except for many gradations of black and white. This had happened unconsciously, and I now realized it was correct. I then deleted most of the few remaining colors, keeping only a few essential ones. I am convinced this helped the story and created an unusual and distinct atmosphere.

After the story's climax, an experience in which the boy suffers shock and disillusion, I had him go to a park and sit on the edge of a fountain. I'm not sure when I realized that the fountain had to be "broken." Maybe during the third rewrite, maybe during the fifth. At any rate, it was right. A beautiful thing, a fountain, had been broken; another beautiful thing, a child's faith, had been broken, too.

Those are a few of the hundreds of decisions about details that went into writing that fairly short piece. Trifles they are, and I certainly would not presume to call any of them magnificent. But each one represented a considered selection. They were added to the story only after I had convinced myself that they served a real purpose.

The "unimportant" paragraph

I have noticed that many writers, myself among them, do their best work when writing the beginning of a piece of fiction and in the dramatic, climactic scenes. Careless use or non-use of concrete details crops up most frequently in an "unimportant" paragraph.

The first place to look for weaknesses is in the scenes that you found less exciting and in transitional passages that you found "easy to write."

When I was fumbling through early drafts of *The Inquisitor's House*, I developed a potentially explosive situation between a crippled father, who had once been an athletic man, and his vigorously active son, a boy just becoming an adolescent. The father, bitterly envious of his son's strength, taunts the youth in many ways. This was a ranch family, and I remember writing the boy's angry outcry against his father. "Why do you force me to ride this old horse when we have a dozen good ones?" The words seemed satisfactory. The passage, at that time, did not seem very important.

During a later revision I suddenly blinked at the expression "old horse." Would a boy who practically lived on horseback use this vague term? Wouldn't he say "old pinto" or "old piebald"? Surely something more definite! Annoyed at my own carelessness, I realized I would have to go over the whole passage with a microscope. If I had been slovenly once in that section, I had probably let slackness creep into other places, too.

Then came the dawn. The "old horse" was a gelding. It had to be! This was the natural insult the envious cripple hurled at his son—the denial of manhood. Why hadn't I seen it before?

The whole passage suddenly began to "exist" for me as I saw new meanings, new envies and hatreds.

I confess I am rather proud of the final scene that "trifle" led me to write. I had thought I was only checking a weak detail, but in doing it I had stumbled upon a whole facet of unexplored character and conflict.

Decisions and choices

In the struggle for good details one learns many things, and for myself I have developed certain self-critical questions. There are dozens of other questions, but these, in general, are the ones I find most helpful:

1. Are you a miser or a spendthrift? Have you crammed the writing with so many details doing the same job that they have lost their meaning? A good detail must not be hemmed in by second-raters. Or is your story so barren that it reads like an outline? Modern fiction tends to avoid both extremes. It reads neither like the cataloguing of early Thomas Wolfe nor the tight-lipped starkness of early Hemingway.

2. Have you used good, meaningful trifles, or merely listed trivialities? If many of the details can easily be cut or others substituted with equal effect, then you're in trouble. If you write, "A birch tree grew in the front yard" and later realize it could just as well be an oak, a poinciana, or a palm, then this tree is probably just overgrowth and you'd better chop it down.

3. Have you examined and re-examined every detail to make sure it is the best possible? If you have written, "Emmy Lou was ironing in the basement," don't just settle for that because it was the first idea that struck you. Did you consciously decide that ironing was the best activity, or did you just give poor Emmy something to do, thinking that ironing was easier than hauling clinkers out of the furnace? Don't dismiss it because Emmy is an unimportant character and what she's doing is "just an unimportant trifle." In such a dismissal you may be losing an opportunity to be magnificent!

4. Have you tolerated generalities? Fiction deals with the concrete, and usually with the exact. The question just asked is of utmost importance. Consider the following three statements:

(a) The four men played cards on Tuesday nights.
(b) The four men played poker on Tuesday nights.
(c) The four men played Old Maid on Tuesday nights.

"Cards" is a meaningless generality unless you go on to explain that sometimes it was one type of game and sometimes another. The other two statements give a definite picture. In other words, they are concrete and therefore *meaningful.*

You have a woman wearing "a flower." Was it an orchid or a tea rose or a daisy? Or a man buys "a magazine." Did he buy *Stag, Business Week,* or *Variety?* Such details count. Eventually they add up to a character—and a world.

In revising your manuscript check, double-check, and then triple-check for generalities such as "cards," "a magazine," "a drink," "a book," "music," "a painting," and hundreds of others. If you uncover a great many of these in your work, you must go back and start over. Your thinking has been wrong; you have not visualized the concrete details of your scenes.

There will be times when you choose to say "a painting" instead of "a portrait" or "an abstract." You may decide not to tell whether the "drink" was a lemonade or a martini. But it must be a deliberate decision, not a generality that you failed to notice.

From all this you have gathered that I am a fanatic about the small things, the details of writing. Well, I am! I may be careless about everything else in life, but not about my work. To me, writing fiction is like constructing a Japanese garden: every plant, every stone, every pebble must be examined, selected, and arranged.

Care and labor do not exclude inspiration and excitement. In fact, they are the very extensions of those qualities. A man who is inspired and excited by his work will love it enough to do his best.

It makes no difference whether the writer is struggling with a story that he hopes will have great literary merit, or trying to turn out a blood-and-ambush thriller for *Appalling Adventure Magazine.* The discipline is exactly the same. The trifles that make—or destroy—perfection still must be weighed, measured, considered. No one who calls himself a writer can afford to do otherwise.

~ 15 ~

FINDING YOUR VOICE

TODAY's new world of fiction offers an endless challenge. Never has the art been so free in its forms and open in its range of possibilities.

None of us—neither you nor I—will ever write as well as we would wish to write. We will not always find the trifles that make perfection, and maybe perfection is unattainable for any writer. It could well be that quality that is always beyond the best of what the best of us can do.

We all dream of capturing the magnificent details that will reveal truth in a confused world, that will cast light in the darkness that surrounds all of us.

The struggle for excellence—even a small degree of it —is a hard battle. But it is worth the effort—worth all of it! Some fiction writers claim, almost contemptuously, that they "write only for money." That may be true at certain times in their lives. I am convinced this was never their real intention. One writes in search of reality and truth because one *must* do it. It is a special burden and a special joy.

Why does a fiction writer keep working? The best explanation I know comes from a strange source. In *The Children of Sanchez* the late Oscar Lewis quoted an ignorant Mexican slum-dweller, a man without hope whose life has been nothing but a series of disasters and mistakes. This man, Manuel, says that he will die leaving no trace of himself behind, "like a worm dragging itself across the earth."

Manuel finds it "laughable" that a man so ignorant and hopeless as himself should feel an impulse to write. But then he tells why we all continue the struggle: "I would like to sing the poetry of life . . . great emotions, sublime love, to express the lowest passions in the most beautiful way. Men who can write of these things make the world more habitable; they raise life to a different level."

Let's assume that you are a young author, young in ambition and imagination, whatever your actual years, and you are about to enter the field of fiction. When you look at the landscape you hope to conquer, you will see a varied and bewildering world.

The term "fiction" is so broad that we will make no attempt to fence it in with a strict definition. It is an area of literature vast enough to contain Elsie Dinsmore and Myra Breckenridge, to encompass Portnoy and Huck Finn. In modern fiction, outright pornography co-exists with religious stories designed for our moral salvation. We have confessions, juveniles, mysteries, humor, realism, science, social reform—something for every taste.

An outsider would think that fiction published in something called *Avant-Avant Literary Forward* would have nothing whatever in common with stories in *Sexy Tales for Males*. A writer knows that these magazines are not so utterly different as they seem at first glance. Both of them, in very distinct ways, demand a story that catches and holds a reader's attention; both seek work that grips the emotions and imagination. Further, the distinctions that once sharply separated "literature" from "popular trash" become increasingly blurred as the general level of education improves.

Although all types of fiction tend to follow the same general principles of sound narrative writing, it is obvious that there are different fields in the world of storytelling. In which of these fields should you try to stake out a claim? Are you a "serious novelist" or a wry creator of light entertainment?

Most young writers have an immediate answer to such a question. "I'm going to write wistful, tragic, sensitive novels about my unhappy childhood. Pulitzer Prize works," says one. And another: "Science fiction's my bag, man!"

I feel skeptical of these snap decisions. The average beginner has not yet found his voice—he doesn't know if he is a lyric soprano or a basso profundo.

The grim realist who struggles futilely to create a successor to *An American Tragedy* may at heart be a new Hans Christian Andersen. Rex Stout, before he evolved the famed armchair sleuth Nero Wolfe, was a very serious novelist indeed. He was also successful, insofar as the fact of publication marks success. But his career did not soar until he found his true voice in the field of mystery fiction. Tennessee Williams wrote a novel and a number of short stories which attracted only a limited audience. His true voice was that of a playwright. A friend of mine completed six mystery novels, because "mysteries are the best bets for newcomers." All six were rejected. After turning away from this "best bet," she has had several stories printed by literary magazines. This woman has an authentic talent for literature, but minimum ability in the suspense field. She knows this now, but five years ago believed the opposite.

The list of misdirected efforts would be increased a thousandfold if we knew the names of all the talented and hopeful writers who gave up in despair after failure in only one or two fields of fiction writing. The potential author must realize that it is possible to misunderstand the nature of his own ability. In launching your own career in fiction, try not to specialize too early.

"But I have to start somewhere! Surely no one writer can be expected to write every type of fiction!"

True enough. Most professional authors do not leap from field to field—although some do—and changing a style is not as easy as changing a shirt. I think there is only one writer who can and should produce every type of fiction: the complete beginner.

An apprentice can afford to experiment. He has no literary reputation to lose, no following of readers who expect certain things from his work.

Allow me to be briefly autobiographical. When I decided to become a fiction writer, I was uncomfortably aware that I could not afford an overly long apprenticeship. Time was money, and of money I had little. Unless I enjoyed rather quick success, my dream of writing fiction would be doomed or at least long deferred.

During those first desperate months, I worked sweatshop hours on a strict schedule. I had to confine myself to short stories, because the time for writing a novel was out of the question. But, except for a novel, I wrote *everything*.

What followed is not a rags-to-riches saga. I was not in tatters then, and I am not now dictating these words to a svelte secretary while lolling on the deck of my luxury yacht! But I did enjoy a measure of success very quickly, and I have survived as a fiction writer.

At the beginning, such survival was possible only because I knew I was on unfamiliar seas and I had to cast out lines in every conceivable direction. My first three publ'shed stories appeared in *The Atlantic, Ellery Queen's Mystery Magazine,* and the confession publication, *Modern Romances.* An odd record, I suppose, although many other writers have done much the same thing. (At the time I did not think it strange. I rejoiced briefly at each acceptance, raced to the bank, then raced back to my typewriter.) I do not think those early sales reflect versatility so much as they reveal a great deal of groping about and the writing of thousands of words: I was trying to find my voice, to discover where I fitted in.

Some early surprises taught me that a novice is a poor judge of his own work and his own potential. I felt supremely confident that I could write acceptable science fiction. But my attempts were so terrible that I never even finished a story in this field. However, the time spent in trying was not wasted: I learned more about narrative writing and more about myself.

I was convinced that I could write hard-boiled adventure tales, and equally certain that I had not the technique demanded by the publications foolishly lumped together as "the slicks." No one could have been more mistaken. A story called "Evening at the Black House" was to be my assault on the tough-guy magazines. But no editor of such a publication ever saw it. Thanks to a shrewd literary agent, the piece was taken by *Cosmopolitan* and has since enjoyed international reprinting in anthologies. So much for my early assessment of my own work and my assessment of "the slicks"!

Although the case history of one writer cannot be applied to all others, I believe a few general truths may be drawn from my trial-and-error method:

First, a beginner should try his hand at every type of story, and *all at once.* I do not mean you must have manuscripts in three typewriters and leap from one machine to the next. But as soon as you have completed a work for a literary magazine, start on a suspense story or a science fiction tale or whatever else comes to mind. (The obvious exception is when you have an idea that "just begs to be written.") Do not say to yourself, "I will devote this year to trying *The New Yorker, The Atlantic,* and *Harper's.* If that fails, next year is for science fiction and the following year . . ." Such a resolution is dangerous because it may breed despair while time is wasted. You may give up before you reach the one field that is best for you.

Second, renounce all literary snobbishness. It is presumptuous and unrealistic to think you can begin at the top. Since you are a newcomer, there is no magazine so humble that it does not merit your attention. Somerset Maugham described the reactions of some narrow-minded pedants to a brilliant colleague by saying, "They could not think a man profound whose interests were so diverse." Versatility is not a mark of shallowness.

The most hopeless young writers I meet—except for the non-writing dabblers—are the snobs who, though unpublished, presume to talk about "contributing to literature" and "creating art." Art is an angel that the craftsman entertains unawares, and I cannot imagine St. Cecilia saying, "Well, sisters, today I think I'll play the organ and draw a cherub down." These brash beginners are determined that their work will be at least as revolutionary as *Ulysses,* and they conveniently forget that James Joyce first mastered his craft by writing the powerful but conventional stories of *Dubliners.*

These same people haughtily say, "If I can't be a major author, a true artist, then I don't want to write at all." But most great writers became "major" only after producing a quantity of minor and often unpublished work. Craft must be learned before art can be dreamed of, and a beginner can seldom guess his own potential. Part of finding your voice is discovering whether you have the ability to become a prima donna or merely a chorus singer.

Another form of snobbery involves the word "commercial." Some novice writers think that "commercial" is the dirtiest adjective in the literary lexicon. Is it really so wicked for a writer to try to earn a living? William Faulkner wrote *Sanctuary* "to make money." Dr. Samuel Johnson, always given to extreme statements, declared that "Only a blockhead ever wrote anything except for money." Dr. Johnson is a bit absurd, but I suppose if he had put all the necessary modifiers in his remark (God forbid!), it would not have been pithy enough to be quotable.

However, *all* writers hope to make money—or at least to reach an audience, which comes to the same thing. But there is one "commercial" attitude which can threaten your work. The writer who labors over a story—or, worse, a novel—that bores him, struggling to produce something he knows is cheap and contemptible, is usually doomed to both literary and commercial failure. The lack of excitement and integrity will come through to the reader loudly and clearly. You may be well aware that the field you are working in has literary limitations, but you must be sincere and excited about the particular piece *while you are writing it.* It is difficult to type with one eye on your manuscript and the other on a cash register.

Third and last: During the period of finding your voice, never look upon a rejected work as a failure. It is simply a negative experiment, an attempt you had to make as part of the process of self-discovery. And self-discovery is the beginning of all careers in fiction writing.